SECRETS OF THE HEART

Secrets
of the
Heart

Lessons from the Psalms

Stuart Briscoe

Harold Shaw Publishers
Wheaton, Illinois

ISBN 0-87788-767-5

Front cover design and artwork by David LaPlaca.

Library of Congress Cataloging-in-Publication Data

Briscoe, D. Stuart.
    Secrets of the heart : lessons from the Psalms / Stuart Briscoe.
        p.   cm.
    ISBN 0-87788-767-5 (pbk.)
    1. Bible. O.T. Psalms—Sermons.   21. Christian life—Biblical teaching.
I. Title.
BS1430.4.B6767 1999
223'.206—dc21   98-55388
                                                                          CIP

---

03   02   01   00   99

10   9   8   7   6   5   4   3   2   1

Contents

Preface 7

1   The Joyful Heart 9
    Psalm 4

2   The Sorrowful Heart 22
    Psalm 13

3   The Foolish Heart 37
    Psalm 14

4   The Troubled Heart 47
    Psalm 25

5   The Fearful Heart 60
    Psalm 27

6   The Frustrated Heart 72
    Psalm 37

7   The Angry Heart 84
    Psalm 39

8   The Contrite Heart 97
    Psalm 51

9   The Steadfast Heart 111
    Psalm 57

10 The Wise Heart 122
    Psalm 90

11 The Upright Heart 135
    Psalm 119

12 The Humble Heart.....................144
    Psalm 131

Preface

Living in a society where our external image is highly valued, we need to be reminded that what ultimately matters from God's perspective is what is going on in our hearts.

I've discovered that the Bible is an excellent book on this subject of the heart. It wasn't until I had been preaching for more than twenty years at our church—with brief intervals for eating and sleeping—that I finally got around to explaining what the Bible says about this often-mentioned organ. To my utter amazement I found that the heart is referred to almost 1,000 times!

However, I will narrow this study of the heart to focus on the book of Psalms. This book is known as the hymnbook of Judaism and is clearly an area of Scripture in which God's people respond to him from their innermost feelings and desires. The Psalms contain many references to the heart, all of which reveal the inner dimensions and dynamics of a person relating to God in all of life's ups and downs—something we all should learn to do.

1
The Joyful Heart
Psalm 4

The brilliant seventeenth-century French mathematician Blaise Pascal was deeply interested in theology. When he wasn't working out highly complicated algebraic formulae, he did a lot of thinking about issues of faith and reason. He hoped to write a book about the spiritual life, so he scribbled little notes to himself on bits of paper anywhere and everywhere, some of them actually sewn inside his coat. Unfortunately, he died before he ever wrote the book, but it would have been fabulous. We know because the random notes he made have been put into a book titled *Pensées*, or "thoughts." The thoughts of Blaise Pascal are well worth reading sometime.

One thought from his book is the well-known phrase "The heart has its reasons." I think Pascal's point was that sometimes there are reasons for our behavior and attitudes that we don't always recognize. Certainly there are things going on inside us that we don't always admit. For example, a young man's strident atheistic statements may sound intellectual but may actually spring out of a deep heart-hurt. When the man was a boy, his father was killed and some well-meaning soul said, "God loved your Daddy so much that he took him to live with him." The young man's heart has its reasons for denying that God.

We can often give a rationale for our actions. We can explain why we have done this, that, or the other, which may or may not be true. It depends on whether we recognize and admit that the heart does have its reasons.

External or Internal?

In this culture we tend to be externally oriented when we really need to be more concerned about the inner person. We are encouraged to dress for success, to make a good first impression, to project the right image. Politicians know this and often hire "image-makers." They set up photo opportunities in order to project an image—one that conveys a message that may or may not be true.

We aren't the only people into externals. The children of Israel insisted on having a king, an external leader. God was much more into a theocracy than a monarchy, but eventually he told Samuel that he could go ahead and find them a king. Saul, handsome and strong, was the first king that Samuel anointed. But he was eventually rejected by God. As Samuel looked for the next king, God warned, "Don't look on the outside, Samuel; look on the inside. Man looks on the outer appearance, but I look at the heart." Why? Because the heart has its reasons, and it's the inner person that really matters. Even though we might be more interested in externals, God is more interested in *eternals.*

In the New Testament, the Pharisees were very much concerned about externals in religion and being ceremonially clean. The Lord Jesus told them, "It's not what goes into you that defiles a person. It's what comes out of you. It's the heart that defiles." The Old Testament doesn't have a very complimentary view of the heart either. It says the heart is deceitful above all things and desperately wicked. So we need to be concerned about our hearts, about what is going on inside of us.

Another brilliant Frenchman who lived in the nineteenth century was Alexis de Tocqueville. He visited the United States and then wrote his famous two-volume work, *Democracy in America*. It's full of observations that politicians and others love to quote, though very few people have actually read the book. One thing that de Tocqueville noticed about this burgeoning sociological experiment called the United States of America was that there were unique behavior patterns in the Americans. He traced these patterns to what he called "the habits of the heart." In other words, what was going on in this sociological experiment was directly attributable to what was going on *inside* the people. It was the habits of their hearts that made the difference in their actions.

The point is rather obvious. We don't need Frenchmen to tell us the significance of the inner person, though we're grateful for Blaise Pascal and Alexis de Tocqueville. What ultimately matters from God's perspective is what is going on inside our hearts.

A Greater Joy

The book of Psalms contains dozens and dozens of references to the heart, and we'll begin our study with Psalm 4:

[1]Answer me when I call to you,
    O my righteous God.
Give me relief from my distress;
    be merciful to me and hear my prayer.

[2]How long, O men, will you turn my glory into
    shame?
    How long will you love delusions and seek false
    gods?

³Know that the LORD has set apart the godly for himself;
    the LORD will hear when I call to him.

⁴In your anger do not sin;
    when you are on your beds,
    search your hearts and be silent.
⁵Offer right sacrifices
    and trust in the LORD.

⁶Many are asking, "Who can show us any good?"
    Let the light of your face shine upon us, O LORD.
⁷You have filled my heart with greater joy
    than when their grain and new wine abound.
⁸I will lie down and sleep in peace,
    for you alone, O LORD,
    make me dwell in safety.

Notice what is being said here, particularly in verse 7: "You have filled my heart with greater joy than when their grain and new wine abound." In the culture in which the psalmist lived, the harvest times of grain and new wine meant that the basic commodities of life were being provided. This psalm recognizes that material blessings *can* bring a certain measure of joy. But there is no shortage of people in this world who have an abundance of material blessings but do not have riches of joy. In fact, some of the unhappiest people on the face of God's earth are those who are the most materially enriched.

Harvest time was also a time of great celebration. It was party time, for the hard work of the farming was done. But Psalm 4 proclaims that there's a greater joy than you can ever receive from material blessings or from "party time." And the source of this joy? "You [LORD] have filled my heart with greater joy."

The psalmist is not pretending that life is easy. In fact, he speaks openly about the disappointments and the discouragements of life. It was in the midst of these difficulties that he discovered a fullness of joy and a peace so deep that he was able to enjoy being awake and he was able to get a good night's sleep.

This psalm falls naturally into three divisions. First, the psalmist is talking to God in prayer. Then he talks to society and begins to address people and their heart needs. In the third part, he talks about the fact that the Lord is pouring blessings into his life. Let's look at each of these areas more carefully.

Approaching God in Prayer

Most of us would say that we believe in prayer. But if we're strictly honest with ourselves, is it possible that we believe in prayer without being particularly adept at it? Is it possible that we believe in prayer without being very committed to it? Is it possible that we believe in prayer without instinctively turning to it?

Have you ever watched professional athletes and said to yourself, "They make it look so easy. I could do that"? Then have you ever gone out and tried to do it yourself and wondered how in the world they can make it look so easy? You and I can feel like klutzes trying it ourselves. Obviously, professional athletes have natural abilities, but in addition to such gifts, they must practice and practice and practice and practice. When the time comes to perform, the body has been programmed. The mind is ready; instinct takes over.

So it is with prayer. You don't wait till the roof falls in to figure out how to learn to pray. You don't humble and bumble through prayer only when disaster hits. You develop a relationship with the Lord that has an integral part called prayer. Notice what the psalmist tells us about prayer that we must learn.

1. Address the right person.
You can pray with great enthusiasm and with tremendous

fervency to someone or something that cannot hear or answer your prayers. According to verse 2, there are many false gods and delusions. The key to effective prayer is not so much its earnestness and its fervency, but the One to whom it is directed. Is there a God who hears and answers prayer? Is there a God who is able and willing to do something about it?

The psalmist is very clear on this point. The whole psalm is addressed to the LORD, printed in all uppercase letters. This reminds us that he is praying to Jehovah—the great name by which God has chosen to reveal himself. It speaks of his eternal nature. It speaks of his self-sufficiency. It speaks of the fact that he is without beginning and end. It speaks of the fact that he is the One who has chosen to reach out to us and develop an intimate relationship with us, given his utter holiness and transcendence. It is the mysterious, wonderful name whereby God reveals his character and nature to us. This great God is the One to whom we pray.

There probably aren't very many people who could fly to Washington, D.C., jump in a cab to the White House, go straight through the gates because they're recognized, walk through the corridors to the Oval Office, knock on the door, walk right in and say, "How are you doing, Mr. President? How's it going?" Why, then, do we feel we can casually wander into God's presence when we feel like it? "Hey, God, how's it going? By the way, here's my shopping list. Do this. Do this and this. And I want to know, why didn't you do that? And I'm upset about this. And I think you should have done that."

Notice how the psalmist begins: "Answer me when I call to you, *O my righteous God.*" Perhaps a better translation might be, "O God of my righteousness." When we barge into God's presence on our terms and demand that he do what we expect him to do, we're speaking out of our supposed righteousness. We have the feeling that we have the right to question God; we have the right to demand of

God. We are acting like there's something intrinsically righteous about us that allows us to go into his presence like that. What is God's reply? "You have it all wrong, folks."

There is no basis in your righteousness that allows you to move into the presence of God. You must admit that your righteousness is as filthy rags, repent of your unrighteousness, and receive the incredible gift of forgiveness in Christ. When I discover that God is the One who provides me with righteousness, that he is the God of my righteousness, then I have the basis upon which I can come before him in prayer.

Humbly. Gratefully. Thankfully. We say to him, "O God, I'm not coming on the basis of my righteousness; I'm coming to you, the God of my righteousness."

2. Respond with the right attitude.

The psalm moves on to say that the Lord has "set apart the godly for himself" (vs. 3). Who are the godly? What is a godly person? Let's look at the basis for godliness.

There's a wonderful Hebrew word that is common in the Old Testament, *hesed,* which describes the character of God. It is translated as "loving kindness," "tender mercies," or "faithful love." It describes how God deals with us gently, kindly, graciously, lovingly, and faithfully. He has demonstrated all these things to us in a thousand ways.

Related to *hesed* is another word, *hasid* or "godly." If *hesed* is a description of the character of God, *hasid* describes the people who respond to that part of God's character. What would be an appropriate response, then, to the loving kindness and tender mercies of a faithful God? Loving, faithful commitment to the God of lovingkindness, demonstrated in a generosity of spirit to those to whom he sends us.

Who are the people who can move easily into God's presence in prayer? They are those who say, "I come before you, Lord, not on the basis of my righteousness, but on the basis of your loving kindness demonstrated to me in

Christ. I come as a forgiven sinner whose heart is moved to love and to obey you faithfully. Responding to your *hesed*, I come before you as somebody who is delighted to be set apart by you for yourself. I lay myself before you in humble, expectant prayer." When a person comes before the Lord with that kind of an attitude, God finds it relatively easy to fill our hearts with a greater joy than we will ever know from the "grain and wine" of material things.

3. Ask the right things.

When we come to God in prayer, what do we ask him? Fortunately, verse 1 gives us some ideas: "Answer me when I call"; "Give me relief"; "Be merciful"; "Hear my prayer." Does God hear and answer?

When I travel for any length of time, I return to a desk piled with letters. But catching up on correspondence is not what really bothers me. It's that little red light that blinks on my phone, telling me that messages are waiting for me. My machine is fixed so that you can only get twenty-five messages on it. I was told that, if I wished, it could be extended to 100. I do not wish. I know that I'm going to pick up that phone, and the irritating voice of that lady inside the phone will say, "You have twenty-five messages waiting for you." It usually takes me quite a while to return all twenty-five.

I've got great news for you. God's phone mail blinks and he returns his calls. Because you've come to the right Person with the right attitude and asked the right things, he begins to discern what is going to be best for you in terms of his eternal purpose. He doesn't guarantee he'll give you everything you want any more than you would give your children everything they ask for. But he does guarantee that he will impart to you all that is necessary for you to live wisely and well in terms of his great and good and glorious plan for your life.

The psalmist is apparently experiencing some hard times from the people who surround him. One of the things he asks for is relief. "God, people have abused me, people have victimized me, please give some relief," he is saying in effect. The literal word used here is *room*—"Give me some room in these circumstances."

Do you ever feel hemmed in by people and by circumstances or locked into a situation you can't get out of? It is squeezing the life out of you and it has certainly squeezed the joy out of you. Do you know what you do? Make sure that you turn instinctively to prayer. Make sure that you know who you're turning to. Make sure that you come with the right attitude and that you ask him graciously in terms of his good and perfect and acceptable will to give you "room."

In 1994 a remarkable thing happened in South Africa. I have watched events there for almost twenty-five years, and I could hardly believe it as Nelson Mandela was sworn in as president. For twenty-six years, Mandela had been imprisoned. For eighteen of those years, he had lived on Robben Island, a desolate little rock in the middle of Table Bay. I've flown over the island more than once in a helicopter and have seen the spartan circumstances under which he lived. One day a very brave man called F. W. de Klerk came along and set Mandela free, and four years later Mandela became the president of South Africa. There was a man who needed relief, who needed "room," who needed to be set free. And set free, he was then given the opportunity to discover the sheer potential of his life.

That's the kind of relief you can pray for if you're discovering that the joy has been squeezed out of your life. You can come to the Lord—remembering who he is, remembering the basis on which you can come. You can know that he will hear and answer your prayer according to what is best for you.

Living Christianly in a Cynical World

Next the psalmist turns to those who are causing him distress and, instead of being intimidated by them, he begins to challenge them: "How long, O men, will you turn my glory into shame? How long will you love delusions and seek false gods?"(vs. 2). Who are these people who are pressing in on him, ruining his life, victimizing him, and destroying his joy? We know that they're self-sufficient. The word translated "men" should be "great men." These were people of power and authority, men who called the shots.

The psalmist's "glory" was the delight he had in knowing God and knowing that the Lord had set apart the godly for himself. He was glorying in his relationship with God, and these people were denigrating that relationship. So he turns to them and he says, "How long are you going to be self-sufficient? How long are you going to disdain spiritual realities? How long are you going to discount the affairs of the heart? How long are you going to be wrapped up in externals that may not be reflective of the real person?" Then he asks, "How long will you love delusions and seek false gods?" These verses are a commentary on our times as well.

Many of you are having a hard time living "Christianly" in our culture, in your families, in your workplace, because arrogant and self-sufficient people denigrate spiritual realities. They prefer delusions and believe lies rather than the truth. They mock you and reject you. They give you a hard time for seeking to be faithful.

When that happens, come before the Lord in prayer. Discover in him that which will give you fullness of joy that you can't get anywhere else. Then, instead of being intimidated by these people, turn and challenge them: "How long are you going to be self-sufficient, and how long are you going to denigrate spiritual realities, and how long are you going to prefer delusions to truth, and how long are you going to propagate falsehoods that are destroying people's lives?"

Then give them some advice. They may not be asking for it, but give it anyway. Verse 3 can lead you: "You need to know that the Lord has set apart the godly for himself, and the Lord hears when I call on him. You need to know what God is busy doing in our world. You need to know that God has taken an initiative in people's lives. He's touching them, drawing these people to himself, and utterly, totally changing them."

My wife, Jill, and I once met a young couple who were singing in the pubs of London. Alex had made his living playing guitar in rock bands; Jenny had come from Australia to make her name in show business. He was a cocaine addict; she had gotten into all the garbage of the rock scene. One day, when Alex offered marijuana to the other guys in the group, they said to his amazement, "We don't do that stuff any more. We've got something better." They talked to him. They encouraged him. They took him to hear Billy Graham, and that night he found Christ, gave up drugs cold turkey and never touched them again. He continued to sing in the pubs, but this time he went back as a believer. He began to communicate, in some of the toughest pubs of east London, the message of Christ's deliverance in his life.

Meanwhile, Jenny was totally disillusioned and desperately lonely. She wandered into a Pentecostal church, where people told her about Jesus. That night she came to faith in Christ. Eventually she and Alex found each other, fell in love, and married. God has utterly transformed their lives.

People who are cynical and skeptical about spiritual realities need to be told, "The Lord is setting apart godly people for himself. You need to know that." We should not be intimidated. We should not allow them to rob us of our joy. We should come before the Lord and find strength in him. We should challenge our culture and tell people to search their own hearts. Look at what the psalmist says here in verse 4, addressing the people who are giving him a hard time: "In your anger do not sin; when you are on your beds, search your hearts and be silent."

People need to know that their own hearts have problems. "Offer right sacrifices," we can say to these people, "and learn to trust in the LORD" (vs. 5).

How significant this psalm is for those who wish to find fullness of joy in difficult circumstances. How much more significant from this base of joy they then go to people who are giving them a hard time and present the goodness of the message of Christ.

Basking in the Lord's Blessing

In the third part of the psalm, the psalmist returns to recounting what God is doing in his life. "Many are asking, 'Who can show us any good?' Let the light of your face shine upon us, O LORD" (vs. 6). The psalmist is referring to the priestly blessing recorded in Numbers 6:24-26:

> The LORD bless you
> > and keep you.
> The LORD make his face shine upon you
> > and be gracious unto you.
> The LORD turn his face toward you
> > and give you peace.

This blessing is often spoken to a couple at the end of a marriage service. We pronounce the blessing and we trust that God is going to do a great work of grace in their lives. Isn't that what people are looking for? Isn't that what people—in their deepest, quietest moments on their beds, when they're on their own and coming to grips with their own hearts—are looking for?

Think of a solar eclipse. The sun is shining in all its glory, and then slowly the light diminishes until, in the middle of a beautiful day, it's suddenly dark and gloomy. What went wrong? Something came between you and the sun. That analogy describes the condition of many people today. Something has come between them and the Lord's grace and joy. Isn't it a tragedy that sometimes people are not able to say that the Lord's face is shining upon them?

Perhaps you too are not experiencing the fullness of joy because you have not come to the Lord in prayer. Perhaps you are not coming to the Lord in prayer because something has come between you and the Son, something so precious that you prefer the doom and the gloom, the eclipse of his light, to the fullness of joy that the Lord offers. Many of my colleagues tell me that, from what they observe in counseling sessions, more and more people seem to be living lives governed by fear. Their motivations come from avoiding the things they're afraid of and building up defenses against them.

I would not criticize anybody for being fearful in this world of ours. I've been around it a time or two, and there's some pretty fearsome stuff going on! But a person who knows how to come rightly before the Lord, to trust him, and to ask the right things of him can assume a fullness of joy and can also experience a tranquility of heart and spirit. They can get a good night's sleep. The psalmist knew it firsthand: "I will lie down and sleep in peace, for you alone, O LORD, make me dwell in safety."

Remember, it's the heart that matters. Search your own heart and ask yourself honestly, Is my heart at peace? Do I experience fullness of joy? God offers joy that is fuller and richer than even the abundance of grain or new wine can provide. Trust him and you will find him to be utterly faithful.

2

The Sorrowful Heart

Psalm 13

Many people have their own special sorrows and assume they are alone in them. Perhaps you are under such a burden of concern and grief that you really do not want to go anywhere—least of all church. You cannot face the crowds, and you cannot face the music. You cannot face the thought of all those happy people, and you assume you would feel totally isolated. You imagine you would feel like a turtle on a fence post; "I'm just going to stand out," you say. You want to stay home and stay with your sorrow. Going to a place of worship and being with God's people, however, would be a good thing for you. Let's see why.

Psalm 13 is a very personal lament. The author, David, is complaining about his own specific sorrows. But notice that, having written this song about his own life, the psalmist then gave it to the "director of music." The director of music decided that this was something that the whole congregation should share in, not just the individual who wrote it. So it was incorporated in the psalter, or the book of Psalms, and became part of the corporate worship experience.

You may ask, "Why would a whole crowd of people want to sing or recite something that one person was feeling?" I think there are two obvious answers to that. First, many people will identify with the experience and be able to articulate their own feelings more clearly. Second, if the whole congregation begins to recite or sing these words, they perhaps will understand how other people are feeling. They will begin to get a sense of what is going on in other people's lives. So we will take the psalms, even ones like this that are individual laments, and share them corporately as God's people.

Let us look at Psalm 13:

1How long, O LORD? Will you forget me forever?
  How long will you hide your face from me?
2How long must I wrestle with my thoughts
    and every day have sorrow in my heart?
  How long will my enemy triumph over me?

3Look on me and answer, O LORD my God.
    Give light to my eyes, or I will sleep in death;
4my enemy will say, "I have overcome him,"
    and my foes will rejoice when I fall.

5But I trust in your unfailing love;
    my heart rejoices in your salvation.
6I will sing to the LORD,
    for he has been good to me.

This psalm falls very naturally into three sections. The first part forms a sorrowful complaint (vss. 1-2), then comes a prayerful response (vss. 3-4), and the third pair of verses become a joyful conclusion (vss. 5-6). From a position of deep sorrow, chagrin, and complaint the psalmist moves to a place of deep worship and joy. What starts out as a sorrowful heart finishes, in the brief space of six verses, as a singing heart.

Some may argue, "You can't deal with your sorrow and issues that quickly. This sounds like escapism." I agree; it does sound like that. No, we're not going to solve all our problems in the space of six brief verses, but we can enunciate some principles that we can apply in our own lives.

The Sorrow of Facing Our Mortality

What's the matter with the psalmist? What is his sorrow? We're not told specifically, but we can hazard some inspired guesses as we look at what is written here. Peeking ahead to verse 3, we notice that he is concerned about something he calls "sleeping in death." Many scholars suggest that in all probability the psalmist had been experiencing an ongoing physical problem. Because of this, he had become deeply discouraged and depressed. He may have been looking at the very real possibility that he was going to die as a result of this particular malady. Whether or not he was concentrating on some physical malady, he certainly was confronting his own mortality, and that in and of itself was a concern. People usually do not want to think about death. We have all kinds of ways of avoiding the subject. Unfortunately, sometimes we just cannot get away from it. So the psalmist is looking at the possibility that he is going to finish up dead, and that is a most disconcerting thought to him.

He talks about his "enemy" overcoming him (vss. 2, 4). In Old Testament days people had a different understanding of life after death than we have. The developed theology of death and eternal life given us in the New Testament as a result of the resurrection of Jesus Christ from the dead was not part of their thinking at that time. The Hebrew people tended to think that God's blessing was going to be experienced in the here and now. This, of course, is true, but God's blessing is not exclusively experienced in the here and now. The great hope of the believer is that after the here and now, because Christ is risen, we too will rise with him.

This hope was not as clearly demonstrated to those people in the psalmist's day as it is to us today. Nevertheless, even with the knowledge that we have in New Testament Christianity, the Bible still states that the last enemy to be destroyed is death itself. There's something gross, something obscene, something utterly wrong about death, and it is something that all of us have to face.

The Power of Emotions

A man came to talk to me after a church service. He had been out of work for over twelve months, and it was getting to him. A married couple had been battling infertility for a long time; it was getting to them. I have talked with other people who—in their marriages, in their work situations, in normal material situations living down here on God's green earth—have problems for which they are not finding any answers, and it's beginning to wear them down. Why? Because human beings are not bodies isolated from emotions; neither are we body and emotion isolated from spirit. We are physical, emotional, and spiritual beings. All three are inextricably bound up with each other.

The psalmist also was dealing with a material or physical concern and, as a result, was experiencing some deep emotional problems. Physical ailments can affect you emotionally, and spiritual issues can have a profound beneficial effect on your emotions. We cannot divide ourselves into neat compartments. Consequently, the psalmist has a very deep emotional response to his trauma.

Note that on four occasions he uses the expression "How long?" That's a question all of us have asked in one situation or another. The psalmist was confronted with a never-ending problem, leading him to conclude it was a no-solution situation. All attempts to improve the situation had backfired, and things were just getting worse. He found himself being buried deeper and deeper down into the situation and felt there was no way out.

I know of a woman who has been trying to solve a painful situation in her life. She has been looking for something, yet everything that she has done seems to get her into deeper mire. As a young woman she got married: she walked down the aisle, stood in front of the church, made her promises, and, with all the great desires and longings of her heart, committed herself to marriage. It ended in divorce.

She was deeply hurt by this. But eventually she found another man, and they fell in love. Hope springing eternal in the human breast, as it always does, they embarked on a marriage. It too ended in divorce.

After a period of time, she met another man. She certainly wasn't ready to get into marriage, so she had an affair. The man promised to marry her when he divorced his wife and left his family, so she put all her eggs in the third basket, if you will. Then, to her chagrin, he decided that he couldn't leave his wife and family. When I met her, she was questioning her self-worth. Soon she began to question God. Then she got angry with people and began to get irrational. Eventually she considered suicide.

Do you see how everything compounded itself? See how the situation got deeper and deeper? She was asking, "How long? How long? How long? How long do I have to go through this kind of situation?" Such is the cycle of discouragement.

When Answers Don't Come

Next, the psalmist becomes very confused. "How long must I wrestle with my thoughts?" (vs. 2) he cries. When these unsolved problems come, when these never-ending situations drag on, you begin to lose sleep, you begin to lie awake at night and look at a spot on the ceiling. You go round and round on the same thing; the more you think about the issue, the tighter the spiral becomes. You become more ingrown, more uptight inside, more resentful, and more bitter.

This clearly was the situation as far as the psalmist was concerned. If only somebody would give him some answers, if only somebody would give him some reasons, then the problem would be solved. But it ain't necessarily so.

Søren Kierkegaard, the Danish philosopher and theologian, tells a story of a young boy who was confronting a mathematics examination but hadn't studied for it. So he stole the answer sheet, and he studied all the answers to all the questions. He took the examination and, of course, got an *A*. As Kierkegaard points out, he got all the answers right, but he never solved the problems. We often want all the answers right, but we don't want to have to solve the problems. So we're asking "why?" as we wrestle with our thoughts and go round and round in circles. The answer to the "why" never comes.

In addition to the discouragement and the confusion, not infrequently there's a degree of impatience. The psalmist asks four times, "How long?" He also claims to "every day have sorrow in my heart" (vs. 2). There's no relief. There's no letup in this situation. I get up in the morning and expect it to go away, and it hasn't. *Every day* there's sorrow in my heart, he complains. Impatience is understandable.

We seem to have gotten the idea that we ought not to have sorrow, that we ought to be exempt, that we ought to be immune from these things. One of the great privileges of life in the United States is freedom to pursue happiness. Unfortunately, a lot of people have misinterpreted this into the right to be always happy. I do not believe for a moment that there is an inalienable right for human beings always to be happy. I do believe that there is an unalterable responsibility for human beings to make other people happy, and that's how we become happy ourselves, when people fulfill their responsibility rather than demand their rights.

I believe that happiness is a gracious gift of God. I do not believe it is an inalienable right. If we believe the latter, we will feel cheated and victimized when we're unhappy. We will feel that something has gone sadly wrong with life and that somehow or other we are being abused. "I have no right to be unhappy. I have no right for this sorrow. This thing has got to go," we say. Add to this the fact that we are used to instant gratification and we want everything resolved and done now. Consider the man who prayed, "Lord, give me patience, and give it to me now!"

Given all this, just imagine what is going to happen if morning after morning we wake up with an unsolved situation. Over and over again we have to say, "How long? How long? How long? How long? Every day I have sorrow in my heart." The psalmist is clearly going through deep emotional waters—discouragement, confusion, impatience, and also fear. He is afraid of the sleep of death. He's afraid that his enemies will overcome him. He's afraid that his foes will rejoice. He is afraid that he is going to come apart at the seams.

Has God Forgotten?

Notice that these are very real fears the psalmist is experiencing. Perhaps you have similar fears. Here I am in my situation, you say. It's gone on and on. I've gone round and round. I'm getting myself tighter and tighter inside. I'm becoming discouraged. I'm becoming impatient. I'm becoming confused. I'm becoming fearful. Things are only going to get worse. I just don't know which way to turn.

However, a subtle thing now begins to develop. He cries, "How long, O LORD? Will you forget me forever? How long will you hide your face from me?" (vs. 1). Now the psalmist has a *spiritual* crisis, and that is frequently how it works out. We start with the physical, material concern.

It begins to make a profound impact upon us emotionally. If we do not handle the emotions well and if the physical situation does not change, there is always the possibility that we will slip and slide into a spiritual crisis.

The psalmist thinks the Lord has forgotten him, and he wants to know why the Lord has hidden his face from him. An awful doubt about the goodness and grace of the Lord has come in. If we are not careful, questions such as "Is God really good? Is God really gracious? Why doesn't God do this? If God was such and such a thing . . ." can eventually harden into a belief that God either is fundamentally irrelevant amd unable to do anything or that he does not exist at all.

It is not difficult to see how people slip into this kind of situation. But it is helpful to note that the psalmist actually records for us someone's real experience of sliding into this spiritual crisis. Perhaps this is *your* testimony. The physical and the material affairs of your life have become so traumatic to you that you're emotionally distraught. Because you found no emotional release, you have begun to question the goodness, the grace, or even the existence of God. You're in spiritual crisis.

A Prayerful Response

But look at the turn of events in this psalm. In verses 3 and 4, the psalmist does something that is most appropriate and that people often forget to do: he turns to prayer. He doesn't *say* his prayers; he *turns* to prayer. There's a difference between reciting prayers and knowing what it is to pray.

The key, of course, to prayer is the One to whom we pray. You can pray with great intensity to a block of wood, but it will do you no good at all. It is imperative that we know the One to whom we pray. There is a little phrase here that we might slide over if we are not careful: "Look on me and answer, O LORD *my God.*" Obviously, he's turning to a god, which is a wise thing to do. But which god? One made in his own image? There's no shortage of that kind of god around. The Bible teaches us that God made human beings in his image, and ever since, human beings have been remaking God in their own image. But that is not the way to pray. Pray to the God of revelation, the God of reality, the God of the Bible—who is called "Yahweh, the LORD" and the "God and Father of our Lord Jesus Christ."

When God deals with us, there are two fundamental aspects to his character. These characteristics are both contained in the word LORD (in Hebrew, *Yahweh*). The word *Yahweh* is related to the verb "to be." When Moses asked God what his name was, God gave the enigmatic reply "I AM that I AM." God did not say "I was, I am, I will be." He said "I AM," describing his am-ness, his is-ness. He was describing his eternality and his unchangeableness. He was revealing to us his uniqueness, his total otherness. So one characteristic of God is that he is utterly transcendent, completely different from and other than us.

When we begin to understand God in these terms, the appropriate response is one of awe, reverence, and fear. Some people don't like that word *fear*. They don't think that we should approach God like that today because it was an Old Testament concept, which is banished in the New Testament. Well, I beg to differ.

In the New Testament one of the major criticisms of people is that they have no fear of God. The New Testament encourages us to perfect holiness in the fear of God. The apostle Paul says one of the greatest motivations he has for evangelism is the fear of the Lord. So if we are going to approach our God, it is on the basis of his being an awesome, holy, utterly distinct, totally other, glorious, majestic, eternal, utterly distinct Lord; and we come before him appropriately with awe and reverence and fear.

However—and it's a big however—the other side to God's self-revelation in the name Yahweh is this: he is the covenant-making and covenant-keeping God. Moreover, the remarkable revelation of God in Scripture is that this transcendent, awesome, holy, remote God has taken the initiative and has moved into our lives. He says that he wants to be our Savior, our Lord, our Friend, and our intimate Savior. The transcendent God became incarnate in Christ, lived our life, died our death, rose again, and ascended into the Father's presence. As a result, we actually have access in prayer to the living God.

The basis of this awesome relationship is the sacrificial life and death of our Lord Jesus Christ. How, therefore, can we approach him glibly? How can we approach him casually? We come before him with great confidence, with a sense of holy awe, and we say that, incredibly, this Lord has become *my* God.

It's fascinating to notice the motivation for this psalmist's prayer. He prays, understandably, about fear of the sleep of death. But he also is concerned that his enemies will say, "I have overcome him," and that his foes will rejoice when he falls. In other words, he is deeply worried that people will see him coming apart at the seams and say, "Where is his God? What good did his religion do here?" A major part of the motivation for his praying is a deep concern for the glory of God. He is not just wrapped up with his own personal problems being resolved. There is still a residual respect for the Lord and a desire that he does not behave in such a way that dishonors God.

God's Face Shining on Us

So this person, deeply chagrined, deeply distraught, deeply discouraged, turns to the Lord in prayer. What does he pray? Verse 3 tells us: "Look on me, . . . answer. . . . Give light to my eyes."

In the beginning of this psalm we read, "How long will you hide your face from me?" The psalmist echoes the blessing the priests pronounced on the people, and asks that God would again make his face shine upon him. This comes out of the writer's dark night of the soul. He is discouraged and distraught; he feels that not only is God's light not shining upon him, but God's face is averted from him. He wants to have the sense that God is looking upon him with grace and with kindness.

I was brought up in the north of England in a home connected to a little corner store where my parents made their living. When I went in and out of the house, I had to go by the candy counter. My parents had told me right from the very beginning, "Those sweets are not yours. If you want one, you must ask, and the answer in all probability will be no." So I had to go back and forth past the candy counter looking at those delicious candies, knowing: number one, they weren't mine; number two, I couldn't take them; number three, if I wanted one I had to ask; and number four, it was pointless because they'd say no.

One day the pressure was too much for me. I looked around hurriedly. No one in sight. I whipped a candy into my mouth, and the moment the candy touched my lips I heard the voice of God. Then I realized it was worse than that. It was my father. He had seen me, and his deep voice said, "Stuart, come here." I didn't realize he was just around the corner, and he had some little peepholes through the displays that he'd stacked up there so he could keep an eye on what was going on in the store.

My father used to wear a starched white apron, fresh and clean every morning. He had a big bow tied in the middle. I remember standing in front of him reluctantly, overcome with shame and guilt, staring him straight in the bow. He spoke to me. I didn't want to hear what he had to say. He began to relate to me how I had embarked on a life of thievery, that I was a thief, that if I continued this way I would in all probability become sociopathic. There was a high probability I would finish up in prison. He would have to come and visit me. I remember thinking, "For a candy? Just a little candy?" Anyway, he put the fear of something in me. To the best of my knowledge, I've never helped myself to anything since.

But then he said something else very important. He said, "Stuart, look at me. Look at me." All I could see at that point was this dazzling white, impenetrable, starched barrier. (I've never had any problem with the transcendence and the holiness and the otherness and the distinctness of God. I just think of my father's starched white apron.) Reluctantly my eyes traversed the expanse of his starched whiteness, his glistening purity, until I came to his face. While I heard his solemn words, I detected two things: in the corner of his eye a tear, in the corner of his mouth a smile. My father's "face" was upon me. I wouldn't have missed that for anything.

You can ask that the Lord would not avert his face from you. He will speak straightforwardly and will tell you what you need to know. He won't butter things up. He will tell you exactly what the truth is, but always with a tear in the corner of his eye because he knows your frailty, and with a trace of a smile on his lips because he understands.

As a pastor, people sometimes say to me, "Stuart, you never answer. You don't listen. You won't listen." I have spent interminable hours listening. What they mean is, "You don't agree with us." God will not always agree with you, but he will listen and he will answer. Ask him to give you ears to hear what he is saying.

Knowing God's Goodness

Following the sorrowful complaints and the prayerful response, we are led to the joyful conclusion. Verse 5 gives us an introduction to something quite startling. "But," he says, "I trust in your unfailing love; my heart rejoices in your salvation. I will sing to the LORD, for he has been good to me" (vss. 5-6).

First, the psalmist takes a retrospective look and comes to this conclusion: *God has been good to me.* Have you come to that conclusion when you look back over your life? As a result of his reflection, he says, "I trust in your unfailing love. My heart rejoices in your salvation. You have been good." In the words of Samuel Rutherford,

> I know that there's night and shadows are good for flowers, and moonlight and dews are better than continual sun. So is Christ's absence of special use. And I know that it has some nourishing virtue in it and giveth sap to humility and putteth an edge on hunger and furnisheth a fair faith to put forth itself and to exercise its fingers in gripping it seeth not what.

Now, that may be a little hard to take in because it's in seventeenth-century English, but I was born shortly after that period in England so I love that kind of thing. But notice three things he's saying here. The picture is obvious. Night and shadows are good for flowers. Moonlight and dews are better than continual sun. Sometimes these waiting periods, these seemingly endless "how long?" periods and these "no solution" situations are good for us because in them we learn humility.

We have a tendency to think we're in control. We can do it. And once in a while God allows things to come into our lives, and he taps us on the shoulder and says, "Now who's in control? You certainly aren't." And with that reminder he is being good to you. He's helping you learn humility.

In addition, when you find that the material world and physical circumstances disappoint you, there's a tendency to have a hunger for something more. God is being good to you in allowing you the opportunity for humility and hunger. Moreover, when you find that these interminable situations never end, you have your hope in something else. If you can learn hope and you can learn hunger and you can learn humility, then God has been good to you at that time. The psalmist learned that God is good, and in a retrospective look he rejoices in this truth.

An Eternal Perspective

Second, the psalmist says, "My heart rejoices in your salvation." He anticipates the ultimate reality of his salvation. We are so time bound. We need to be *eternity oriented*. If we can break out of the time bind and become eternity oriented, we will not think so much in terms of how long we have to endure. Rather, we're going to rejoice in our salvation. In his book *Waiting*, Ben Patterson quotes a poem that captures this perspective:

> What you going to do when the river overflows?
> I'm going to sit on the porch and watch her go.
> What you going to do when the hogs all drown?
> I'm going to wish I lived on higher ground.
> What you going to do when the cow floats away?
> I'm going to throw in after her a bale of hay.
> What you going to do with the water in the room?
> I'm going to sweep her out with a sedge straw
> broom.
> What you going to do when the cabin leaves?
> I'm going to climb on the roof and straddle the
> eaves.
> What you going to do when your hold gives way?
> I'm going to say, "Howdy, Lord. It's judgment day."

One thing after another in our lives is being whittled away. What doesn't change? Our eternal home with the Lord. Retrospectively, we see that God has been good to us. Prospectively, we await the final judgment and salvation. That's where it will end.

And what is to be our perspective in between? The psalmist concludes, "I will sing to the LORD, for he has been good to me." How amazing. We can move from a sorrowful heart to a singing heart by simply getting things in the right perspective. We can sing about what God has done and we can lift our voices in glad praise for what he will do. We can sing when we feel like it and when we don't feel like it. Like the psalmist, let's make a decision and tell our sinking spirits, "I *will* sing to the LORD, for he has been good."

3

The Foolish Heart

Psalm 14

Most of us recognize that something is fundamentally wrong with our society. Inner cities resemble battlefields, divorce courts are full, prisons are overcrowded, abortion clinics work nonstop, laws are flouted, leaders are ridiculed. Our disillusionment is palpable. Politicians and sociologists talk about it. Both groups think of all kinds of ways to address the situation. Meanwhile, we look to the government to do something and think that throwing more money at problems will solve them.

The Bible, however, has a unique analysis: the root of these problems is in the individual human heart. It shows us that if the heart is wrong, relationships will be wrong. If relationships are wrong, society will be wrong. If society is wrong, culture will be wrong. Many people do not want to admit that in the human heart resides a fundamentally spiritual problem. Yet, at the root of our vast sociological problems there is a fundamental spiritual issue that needs to be addressed. And that's what this book is all about—

looking at our inner selves and seeing what God needs to change and heal.

Psalm 14 will help us uncover more of the secrets of the heart. It may seem a bit gloomy at first, but we will see that this psalm is not gloomy so much as it is realistic. It was written by David, who was concerned about the evil he saw around him.

> [1]The fool says in his heart,
>   "There is no God."
> They are corrupt, their deeds are vile;
>   there is no one who does good.
>
> [2]The LORD looks down from heaven
>   on the sons of men
> to see if there are any who understand,
>   any who seek God.
>
> [3]All have turned aside,
>   they have together become corrupt;
> there is no one who does good,
>   not even one.
>
> [4]Will evildoers never learn—
>   those who devour my people as men eat bread
>   and who do not call on the LORD?
> [5]There they are, overwhelmed with dread,
>   for God is present in the company of the righteous.
> [6]You evildoers frustrate the plans of the poor,
>   but the LORD is their refuge.
>
> [7]Oh, that salvation for Israel would come out of Zion!
>   When the LORD restores the fortunes of his people,
>   let Jacob rejoice and Israel be glad!

I think the key to understanding this piece of Scripture is found in one of the smallest words in the psalm: "Oh" (vs. 7). Let me explain. You can say the word *oh* in a variety of ways. When somebody explains something to you, you may reply simply, "Oh." Or you can get a bit more excited about it and say with feeling, "Ooohhh." But I think the psalmist is exclaiming even more feeling, "*Oooooohhhh* that salvation would come!" He sees the results of evil around him and he longs for something very deeply, very passionately here.

Where's Your Passion?

Many years ago in England I sang in a choir. One day the tenor who sat next to me said, "I sang in a musical festival last Saturday, the lyric tenor class." When I asked how it went he replied, "Terrible, absolutely terrible. It was about fifty miles away. My car broke down so I had to go on the bus. There was no heating on the bus. I didn't have time to get my breakfast. They had me sing at nine o'clock in the morning. The preliminary rounds of the competition were held in an old schoolhouse, so I had to sing in a little classroom. There were only two people in the classroom: an elderly pianist and an equally elderly judge. I had to sing a Neapolitan love song. Frozen cold, hungry, in this dilapidated building, and I had to sing a Neapolitan love song to these old decrepit folks. When I finished, the judge wrote two words on his sheet."

I asked, "What were the two words?"

He said, "Lacks passion."

A lack of passion was certainly understandable in that case. What is hard to understand is why people so often lack passion about things that really matter. Somebody has said that the church of Jesus Christ resembles a banker's dinner: cold and correct, decorous and dead. Sometimes, however, people get enthusiastic about things, and we call them fans.

Consider, for example, the game of football—what in this country is called soccer. Football is a game in which people apply the foot to the ball. (This is in marked contrast to the American game that bears a similar name. Though it is only when nothing else works that they actually apply a foot to the ball.) Football fans in Europe show their support. They do not stand there politely. They get into it. They get excited. When something really exciting happens, they take off the team scarves that most fans wear and wave them around. They show their passion.

When it comes to spiritual issues, how much passion do you have? Do you utter a polite "oh"? Or a heart-rending "Oooohhhh" like the psalmist's? "Oooohhh, that you would show your glory, Lord, and that salvation for Israel would come!"

The Fool's Heart

"The fool says in his heart, 'There is no God'" (vs. 1). One type of heart problem is denying God's existence. There are different kinds of atheists. There is the philosophical atheist, who would agree with Herbert Spencer's remark, "The infinite cannot be known by the finite." According to this philosophy, it is impossible to know if there is a God, therefore we may as well assume there is no God. It is utterly impossible for human beings to understand and grapple with God. Spencer, however, overlooked one thing: if the infinite chooses to reveal himself to the finite, then it is perfectly possible for the infinite to be known by the finite.

Other people are functional atheists who live their lives as though God is irrelevant. They do not state or necessarily believe that there is no God, but they live as if there is no God to whom they are accountable. Yet those who believe that God is, and those who believe that God isn't, are both taking steps of faith. To believe that God isn't is just as much as act of faith as to believe that God is.

You cannot prove that God does not exist. You cannot say categorically there is no God for a very obvious reason.

The only person who can say categorically there is no God is a person who knows everything, which would include knowing whether or not God exists. But who knows everything?

Let's assume that, on average, each person knows 1 percent of all knowledge. That means we do not know 99 percent of all there is to know. Given this, is it possible that God exists in the 99 percent of all that we do not know? The answer to that is obviously yes. Therefore, we do not take seriously anybody who says categorically there is no God.

If there is no God, there is no Creator. If there is no Creator, you were not created. If you were not created, there is no intelligent purpose or reason behind your existence. If there is no intelligent purpose or reason behind your existence, there is no reason why anybody should regard you as significant or treat you with dignity. If there is no God, anything goes.

The psalmist, however, is not so much concerned about people who say there is no God as he is about people who say *in their hearts* there is no God. There is a difference. The person who says openly, belligerently, and aggressively that there is no God is a philosophical atheist who has come to an intellectual conviction. But the person who thinks or assumes in his heart that there is no God is a functional atheist who simply lives as if God did not exist. There would be no philosophical atheists among the covenant people of Israel whom David was addressing here. But there would be functional atheists, who would simply treat God as if he were an irrelevance to their lives.

Do you know anybody who is a functional atheist? He or she says in the heart but not aloud, "As far as the practical import of this life of mine is concerned, as far as being a human being here on earth is concerned, God is an utter irrelevance. Whether he exists or does not exist is of no interest to me. His commands and his promises are of no concern to me. His offer of salvation and his people are of no interest to me. Worship and prayer have no part in my life."

The problem for such people is that rarely are they honest with what is really going on in their lives. One remarkably honest person was the famous British philosopher Aldous Huxley, who once made this incredible statement:

I had motives for not wanting the world to have meaning. Consequently I assumed it had none and was able without any difficulty to find satisfying reasons for this assumption. For myself, the philosophy of meaningless was essentially an instrument of liberation, both sexual and political.

Huxley had reasons for not wanting God to exist. If there was a God, he would place restrictions on people. Huxley would be accountable; he would be responsible. If there was a God, Huxley could not be his own god. He wanted total freedom in every area of his life, with nobody exercising authority over him. That was the heart reason. Because he did not want a God to exist, it was easy for him to conclude that there wasn't one. He then had no difficulty finding things that boosted his argument—the problem of pain, the problem of evil, the diversity of religions.

The Fool's Despair

Often people who have been operating on the basis that there is no God come to the point of unrelieved despair. They have no hope and no options because, when they look at their lives, they see no rhyme, no reason, no purpose for their existence.

Ernest Hemingway, the great novelist who eventually committed suicide, said, "Life is just a dirty trick from nothingness to nothingness." At least he was honest. If there is no God, there is no judge. If there is no judge, there is no final evaluation of your life. As a result, what you do has no ultimate significance. Why bother worrying about what you do or don't do? If it doesn't matter what you do or don't do, it doesn't really matter if you are or you aren't. People who think they have no Creator simply go from nothingness to nothingness. They are left with a sense of emptiness and feel as if they have been cheated.

Boris Becker, the youngest man ever to win the singles tennis title at Wimbledon, said, "I had it all. I had the fame. I had the money. I had the cars. I had the women. I had absolutely everything, but I had no inner peace. I was only a puppet on a string." Novelist Jack Higgins was once asked, "Now that you're a man, was there anything you wish you had been told when you were a boy that you know now?" He said, "I wish they'd told me when I was a boy that when you get to the top, there's nothing there." Gertrude Stein expressed a similar sentiment: "When you get there, there's no *there* there."

What's the matter with these people? They are simply taking the no-God philosophy to its logical conclusion. They are thinking the thing through and discovering a vast void in their lives.

The Road to Corruption

What a tragedy it is when people live as if God is an ir-relevance. But why should we be concerned? Notice the second half of verse 1: "They are corrupt, their deeds are vile; there is no one who does good." If we operate on the basis that God either does not exist or is an irrele-vance, we must recognize we have nothing to protect us from moral corruption. There is something called evil in the world.

A society or a culture survives because its members hold things in common. Collectively they adhere to certain be-liefs and agree to certain principles. Our culture at least tacitly accepted and abided by certain truths: "Thou shalt not kill. Thou shalt not steal. Thou shalt not lie. Thou shalt not commit adultery. Thou shalt not covet."

If there is an evil, corrupting influence in the human heart, then it is no surprise that we begin to engage in activities that are wrong. And if God is taken out of the picture, who decides what is wrong? Who determines what is moral? Who determines what is immoral? We have basically decided that truth is relative, that there are no absolutes, and that therefore it is entirely up to individuals to do whatever they wish to do. In short, it's nobody else's business.

Where are we today? Why do we have disintegration and fragmentation? Because if you take God out of the reckoning, nothing stems the tide of corruption or defines morality. Nothing determines what is intrinsically, innately good, right, and true, and people do not have the power or the desire to do it. What does the church of Jesus Christ say to moral corruption today? A little "Oh"? Or from the depths of our heart, do we utter a great "Ooooohhh, that the salvation of God would come out of Israel."

God Sees It All

The psalm goes on to say, "The LORD looks down from heaven on the sons of men to see if there are any who understand, any who seek God" (vs. 2). Did you know that there is a divine perspective on the human problem? Were you aware that heaven is observing what is going on here? That is encouraging news and it is frightening news.

God has his eye on what is going on; history is not hopelessly out of control. He also looks on the heart and sees the root causes of the individual's dysfunctional activities and of society's disintegration. Moreover, God evaluates what he sees. God is looking for people who understand and who seek after him.

As the book of Proverbs says, "The fear of the LORD is the beginning of wisdom, and knowledge of the Holy One is understanding" (9:10). The fool is the person who does not choose wisdom, which is predicated on the fear of God—the acknowledgment, the reverence, the commitment to and submission to him. God looks down from heaven and sees the problem: no one is seeking after *him*. Some people may be seeking a god who will help out a bit; others may look for a god to fix their problems and make them feel a bit better. But they are not looking for God to be God, because they want to be their own gods.

Out of this attitude of the heart come all kinds of problems and issues. In verses 3-6 the psalmist refers briefly to aspects of his society that accurately reflect ours. He observes:

- ❐ The universality of iniquity ("All have turned aside")

- ❐ The totality of depravity ("there is no one who does good")

- ❐ The incidence of stupidity ("Will evildoers never learn?")

- ❐ The prevalence of hostility ("those who devour my people")

- ❐ The absence of humility ("who do not call on the Lord")

- ❐ The evidence of insecurity ("overwhelmed with dread")

All these things reflect inner trauma and turmoil. In his book *Bridge Building*, theologian Alister McGrath defines *angst* as "anxiety about losing our way in the vastness of an impersonal world and being reduced to cosmic insignificance, . . . perhaps sheer despair at the bewildering things that threaten to reduce us to nothing more than a statistic—ultimately a mortality statistic."

Hope for Heart Problems

Verses 5 and 6, however, give the fuller picture: "God is present in the company of the righteous. You evildoers frustrate the plans of the poor, but the LORD is their refuge." Here are two glimmers of hope: God is present and he is a refuge.

There is a root spiritual problem and there can only be a spiritual answer. The government cannot answer spiritual problems; legislation cannot truly respond to the human heart. Only the church of Jesus Christ can address the issues and secrets of the heart. Do we honestly believe that the living God—whom people are rejecting and maneuvering into a position of irrelevance—is alive and well in his church? Do we believe that he is a refuge for his people, that men and women can come from all the heartache, disintegration, and disorientation of their lives and find through Christ that which will make their lives make sense?

We see the results of angst, yet in the midst of the world, God has his people. In the midst of his people, God lives and is inviting every person to come and find refuge in him. The church of Jesus Christ is God's answer to what is going on in our world. Unfortunately, the church is often decorous and dead rather than having a passion for God, for our world, and for spreading the good news of the gospel.

May our hearts be open and may we respond with the honesty, hope, and passion shown us in Psalm 14: "Oh, that salvation for Israel would come out of Zion!" And when the Lord restores our "fortunes," let us rejoice and be glad.

4

The Troubled Heart

Psalm 25

One of Job's legendary "comforters" told his suffering friend, "For hardship does not spring from the soil, nor does trouble sprout from the ground. Yet man is born to trouble as surely as sparks fly upward" (Job 5:6-7). That Job received little help from these sentiments is clear from his response, "How painful are honest words! But what do your arguments prove?" (6:25).

I think David would have agreed with Job. In Psalm 25 he offers an honest look at what to do when our hearts are deeply troubled. He is up front, no holds barred, about what is going on in his life. Towards the end of the psalm, he cries out:

> ¹⁶Turn to me and be gracious to me,
> for I am lonely and afflicted.
> ¹⁷The troubles of my heart have multiplied;
> free me from my anguish.
> ¹⁸Look upon my affliction and my distress
> and take away all my sins.

19See how my enemies have increased
 and how fiercely they hate me!
20Guard my life and rescue me;
 let me not be put to shame,
 for I take refuge in you.
21May integrity and uprightness protect me,
 because my hope is in you.

The word *troubles* in verse 17 can be translated as "intense inner turmoil." The psalmist's tough situation has enlarged or expanded. His heart feels as if it is going to burst, and he is afraid it might break. Coupled to that turmoil is an overwhelming, pervasive sense of loneliness. He seems to be saying that he doesn't have any meaningful objectives for his life or any meaningful relationships. Sound familiar to anyone?

A Lonely World

There's no shortage of troubled and lonely hearts in this world. As a pastor, I hear stories daily of people with troubled souls. A man I know has suffered a massive heart attack. He lies in critical condition in the intensive care unit. Imagine the inner loneliness he must feel as he lays there helpless, and the intense turmoil his loved ones are experiencing.

A man goes to work one Monday morning, business as usual. Unexpectedly, he is called in to see his boss, who tells him he is fired and they want his desk cleaned out by noon. His colleagues don't know what to say so they avoid him. He is suddenly experiencing intense inner turmoil and loneliness.

There's a student away at college. She's exhausted, is having difficulty with her classes, and is worried. She wants to come home but is afraid to call her folks. Intense inner turmoil excerbated by a sense of real loneliness.

Another person has just discovered that her mother and

grandmother both died of Huntington's disease. She is being tested now to see if she also has this fatal disease. As she waits for the results, she is going through an intense, lonely inner turmoil which no one can really touch.

We don't always know what to do with lonely people and those going through turmoil. Newspaper columnist Mike Royko once wrote about the fact that the administrators of the city of Chicago had determined that bars should close at 2:00 A.M. instead of at 4:00 A.M. Royko commented that anybody who couldn't get drunk by two o'clock in the morning wasn't going to be helped by two more hours. But one man replied to the column,

> I'm fifty-three years of age and was married for twenty-seven years, and my wife up and left me, just like that. My kids have grown and they're gone. I've got a no-brainer of a job. I drag myself out of bed in the morning, and I go to work; and it is deadly, dull, and excruciatingly boring. I can't wait to get out of work, but I'm in no hurry to go home because there's nothing there.

He said he sits alone in his sparsely furnished apartment and watches television. In desperation he goes to bed, but at two o'clock he wakes up and stares at the ceiling. So he decides to get out of bed and go to a bar. He says, "Don't you dare close those bars because they're full between two to four in the morning with lonely people. Lonely people who are looking desperately for someone to care, someone to relate to."

Intense, inner turmoil excerbated by deep loneliness. Where do we turn?

Faith First

Since this is a longer psalm, rather than looking at it verse by verse, I will give you an overview. Going back to the beginning verses, we find that the psalmist first reaffirms his faith. In the midst of his desperate feelings, there is a residual trust in the Lord:

> [1]To you, O LORD, I lift up my soul.
> [2]   in you I trust, O my God.
> Do not let me be put to shame,
>   nor let my enemies triumph over me.

Many people turn to the Lord last. He is the recourse of last resort after they have tried everything else. In contrast, the psalmist knows what it is to reaffirm his confidence in the Lord, who he believes is worthy of trust. He turned to faith first. And his faith was in God.

When my father was a young man, he helped with a children's Sunday school class. In England in those days they didn't have various classes for Sunday school. They just shoved hundreds of kids into one big room and did what they could with them. One Sunday one of the workers decided he would do something dramatic to get the children's attention. So he put a chair in the middle of the platform and said, "Boys and girls, I am going to demonstrate faith to you. I am going to show you what trust is."

To the intense intrigue of the young people he ran across the platform, leaped high in the air, and landed with a tremendous crash on the chair. Unfortunately, the chair was not equal to the task and splintered in a thousand pieces. He landed flat on his back with his feet in the air. The kids howled with delight. The man was equal to the task, however. He jumped up, brushed himself off and said, "Boys and girls, I intended to teach you one thing, and I have inadvertently taught you two. I tried to teach you about trust and faith, but a second, more important lesson is to be very careful *what you put your trust in.*"

The Father Knows Best

Next we see that the psalmist believes the Lord knows what is best. Look at the promises here:

> 3No one whose hope is in you
>   will ever be put to shame,
>   but they will be put to shame
>   who are treacherous without excuse.

> 4Show me your ways, O LORD,
>   teach me your paths;
> 5guide me in your truth and teach me,
>   for you are God my Savior,
>   and my hope is in you all day long.
> 6Remember, O LORD, your great mercy and love,
>   for they are of old.
> 7Remember not the sins of my youth
>   and my rebellious ways;
>   according to your love remember me,
>   for you are good, O LORD."

Note the emphasis: *Your* ways, Lord; *your* paths; *your* truth. *You* are my Savior and my God. *You* know the way that I should follow. *You* will guide me into truth if I'm willing to learn. *You* will deliver me from trouble if I am prepared to trust in *you*. He then reiterates his belief that the Lord is merciful.

Most of the psalms are written in the context of someone who understands that God has made a covenant with him. A covenant means that God has taken the initiative and said, "I would like very much to be your God, and I'd like very much for you to be my people. I'll prove my faithfulness to you." And God did just that.

He proved his faithfulness to Abraham, to Isaac, to Jacob, and to Moses. He proved it in Egypt, in the wilderness, and in the land of Canaan. He proved it by providing for a vast number of people as they wandered in the wilderness. He proved his faithfulness and his mercy by getting rid of their enemies. So the psalmist looks back at his historical faith and prays, "You have proven your faithfulness, your mercy as of old. Remember to continue to be faithful and merciful to me."

When he thinks of the faithfulness and the mercy and grace of God, the psalmist is reminded of his own waywardness as a young person. He's reminded of the wild oats that he sowed. While he was young he just thought they were wild oats, but now he's realizing that maybe what he's going through now is a wild harvest. We can imagine his conversation with God: "They told me I could sow my wild oats. They never told me I would reap what I sowed. And maybe I need to come to terms with that. O Lord, remember not the sins of my youth. Forgive me for what I've done, because it is just possible there's a connection between what I'm going through now and what I did in those days."

The psalmist continues, "Remember me, Lord. Don't let me slip from your memory. Don't ever allow me to move out of the area of your consciousness. Because you are merciful, don't ever let me be eradicated from the intensity of your concern for me."

I pity people who go through all the vicissitudes of life without having God to turn to. Some of them sit in bars till four o'clock in the morning and go back to empty apartments; others are desperately busy but desperately alone. I do not know how they cope without knowing the Lord.

A Relational God

If we are to know the Lord, if we are to turn to him instinctively and initially in our circumstances, we must learn how we can relate to him and how he relates to us. The psalmist reflects on how the Lord relates to sinners and to the humble.

> ⁸Good and upright is the LORD;
>> therefore, he instructs sinners in his ways.
> ⁹He guides the humble in what is right
>> and teaches them his way.
> ¹⁰All the ways of the LORD are loving and faithful
>> for those who keep the demands of his covenant.
> ¹¹For the sake of your name, O LORD,
>> forgive my iniquity, though it is great.

God relates to sinners.

It's imperative that we understand how God relates to sinners for one very simple reason: sin is one thing that we all have in common. Verse 8 suggests that God teaches sinners about himself: number one, that he is good; number two, that he is upright. Why is it important for sinners to know these two things? Because the Lord is *upright*, that means he is righteous, a straight shooter, holy and separate from sin. Because he is upright, he cannot ignore or excuse our sin. But because he is *good*, he can and he does take an initiative to forgive our sin.

Some people want God to be good; they don't want him to be upright. "Oh, don't worry about it," they say. "God will just forgive you. Everything will come out in the wash. He's a God of love. He's a good God." This totally ignores the fact that God has said that he is separate from sin, that he cannot look upon our iniquity, that he is holy and removed from us, that our sins come between us and our God.

God relates to the humble.

The only way that we sinners can relate to a holy God is to recognize that he is good and come to him in utter humility. We can trust that he "guides the humble in what is right and teaches them his way."

What does it mean to be humble? Winston Churchill had a great political opponent called Clement Attlee, about whom he made many disparaging remarks. To the surprise of everybody, Churchill once said, "Clement Attlee is a very humble man." Then he paused and, with a typical Churchillian twinkle, added, "Of course, he has a lot to be humble about."

That's how I think about myself: I have a lot to be humble about. I could not create myself. I cannot keep myself going. I cannot count on my next breath. I cannot consistently love God with all my heart and my neighbor as myself. I cannot forgive my own sin. I cannot make myself fit for heaven. I can't even convert food into energy for my body. I am incredibly frail, infinitesimal, insignificant, and utterly dependent. I am a speck of dust in a vast cosmos. I am conscious of how much I have to be humble about.

I'm also conscious that my arrogance and pride often prevent me from admitting my frailties. Pride says to God, "I demand this. Why did you do that? I insist you do this. It is my right, God. By the way, if you think you have any rights on my life, forget it. I'm going to paddle my own canoe." The humble person admits that he or she has no claims on God at all but that God has total claims on his or her life.

In the midst of his inner turmoil exacerbated by loneliness, the writer of Psalm 25 turns to the Lord. He does it the only way he can, as a humble sinner reiterating his utter dependence and seeking only the grace and mercy of a covenant God. Only under these terms can God begin to deal with his inner turmoil and loneliness.

A Chosen Way

Psalm 25 speaks of God's covenant relationship and goes on to tell of his guidance in our lives.

12Who, then, is the man that fears the LORD?
   He will instruct him in the way chosen for him.
13He will spend his days in prosperity,
   and his descendants will inherit the land.
14The LORD confides in those who fear him;
   he makes his covenant known to them.
15My eyes are ever on the LORD,
   for only he will release my feet from the snare.

Those who are in a covenant relationship with the living God and have responded to his offer of grace and mercy understand that God has a way chosen *for them*. The apostle Paul speaks of this truth in Ephesians 2:8-10: "By grace are you saved through faith; . . . Not of works lest any man should boast. For we are his workmanship created in Christ Jesus unto good works, which God has before ordained that we should walk in them" (KJV). I remember a song from my childhood titled "There's a Work for Jesus That Only You Can Do." My hair used to stand on end as I thought about how a path was chosen for *me*. He has a work for you as well. What a wonderful truth.

In this psalm, we see a person with a troubled heart, alone in intense inner turmoil. But one thing he does not forget: as he comes before God humbly, God is going to teach him and lead him in the path chosen for him. Gradually, the psalmist may even be able to affirm that—dare we say it?—maybe the dark days were chosen.

St. John of the Cross, a sixteenth-century mystic and poet, talked about the human experience of the "dark night of the soul." He said that these times of grief, affliction, and loneliness were "the knocks and rappings at the door of [the] soul that it might love more, for they cause more prayer and more spiritual sighs to God." This rings true, for when everything is smooth and easy, we live at a certain level. But problems get our attention. When we discover the inner turmoil of the soul, we begin to pray.

We are driven to God and can turn to him. We begin to have a newness and a freshness of relationship with him.

Sometimes we cannot pray. I heard about a boy who was in trouble. He said to his father, "I can't pray, Dad." His dad said, "Well, just groan." Just groan. The Spirit of God will take the groans of the intense inner turmoil of your heart and translate them into fragrant prayers in the presence of God. And our God hears and answers.

Trusting the Covenant God

Perhaps you too are saying, "The troubles of my heart have multiplied." Have you come before God reaffirming your utter confidence in him? Are you living in a happy relationship with him, one of trust and obedience? Verse 10 reminds us, "All the ways of the LORD are loving and faithful for those who keep the demands of his covenant." This offer of grace—whereby God takes the initiative, reaches out, and gives us what we don't deserve—has another side to it. We are to live in glad, loving obedience to him.

This is not simply Old Testament theology; remember what Jesus said in the Great Commission of Matthew 28:19-20. He told us to go into all the world, making disciples and teaching people to obey everything he had commanded. Who discovers in the dark night of the soul the richness of God's blessing? Those people who not only trust the covenant God but also obey the demands of the covenant in the power of the Spirit. They live through the troubled times, humbly trusting and carefully obeying, even when that's the last thing they want to do.

As the psalmist thinks about this covenant, he suddenly goes back to that old theme that seems to be underlying his concern. "For the sake of your name, O LORD, forgive my iniquity, though it is great" (vs. 11). He is not saying necessarily that there is a direct cause-and-effect relationship between the sins of his youth and the problems he's going through now. Sometimes the hard things that we're experiencing now are the product of human fallibility or of the fallen culture and society of which we are a part. We should, therefore, be careful before we make the direct link.

But we should always be prepared to examine our own hearts and ask, "Could it be that this intense inner turmoil, this sense of loneliness, this sense of estrangement from the Lord is because I am going on in my sin? I go to church, I read the Scriptures, yet deep in my heart I have no intention of changing. Is this why my heart feels cold?"

When Feelings Overwhelm

Some of us tend to live only in our brains, and others live only in our feelings. God gave us both, so let's try to balance them out. Notice the feelings that the psalmist reveals:

- ❐ Feelings of aloneness: "Turn to me and be gracious to me, for I am lonely and afflicted" (vs. 16).

- ❐ Feelings of tension: "The troubles of my heart have multiplied; free me from my anguish" (vs. 17).

- ❐ Feelings of unworthiness: "Look upon my affliction and my distress and take away all my sins" (vs. 18).

- ❐ Feelings of uncertainty: "Guard my life and rescue me; let me not be put to shame" (vs. 20).

If you are living in the area of your feelings, to whom do you turn with such feelings? Do you know the Lord whom the psalmist describes? Through his Son, Jesus, God made a covenant with you that he would be your God, forgive your sin, and give you a new heart and a desire to keep his commands. He promised he would send his Spirit into your life. Do you know him? Are you able to live in an ever-deepening relationship with him? Are you discovering that even the dark times of the soul are leading you to prayer and dependence on him that is enriching your life beyond your wildest dreams?

If you turn to God, you will be discovering some other feelings as well, including *hope*. In verse 21 we read, "May integrity and uprightness protect me, because my hope is in you." The integrity and the uprightness of which he speaks could be the attributes of God, like the bulwarks of his faith. They are the pillars upon which everything is built. Or it could be that, because of God's work in his life, he has become an upright person and a person of integrity. Even in the midst of his turmoil, he's still a person of integrity and is still living rightly before the Lord.

A New Focus

This psalm is an acrostic poem, a clever technique of Hebrew poets in which each verse begins with a different letter of the Hebrew alphabet in alphabetical order. Verse 22, however, was stuck on the end and is not part of the acrostic.

This psalm comes from a broken heart, so perhaps in verse 22 the psalmist is saying, "Ooops. I got myself so absorbed in my difficulties that I spent all the time praying about my troubles, my needs, and my longings. I just remembered something: there's a world of need out there." Instead of ending his prayer with the troubles of his heart, he says, "Redeem Israel, O God, from all their troubles too!"

There's a spiritual truth here. If, in the intense inner turmoil and loneliness of your heart, you know to turn to the Lord first and discover a deepening and a renewing of your relationship with him, you will discover that inevitably *he turns your eyes outwards to those in need.* Then you will find that the answer to your problems and the alleviation of your pressures is found not only in your relationship with the Lord but also in your committing yourself to be of service in his name to others in need.

I read recently about a reporter who asked a young child lying in a hospital suffering from cancer this incredible question: "What is the purpose of life?" The little child did not miss a beat and said, "I think the purpose of my life is that God allowed me to get cancer and I think he may help me to get better. And if he does, it will be so I can be a doctor who works with people who have children with cancer. And when they say to me, 'You don't know what it's like,' I'll be able to say, 'Oh, yes I do because I had it myself.' And I think that's the purpose of my life."

Can you imagine a little kid traumatized with cancer thinking his experience through like that? Have you addressed the intense inner turmoil of your heart? Do you know to turn to the Lord for sustenance, and then to look outward to others in need? This is the way to cope with a troubled heart.

5
The Fearful Heart
Psalm 27

Grace Isaacs had it all—beauty, talent, intelligence. She dated the big man on the Cambridge campus, David Sheppard, who was a world-class cricketer in the 1950s. He shocked the British sporting community when he announced that he was turning away from his athletic career in order to go into the Anglican ministry and commit himself to a ministry in one of the poorest neighborhoods of London.

David married Grace, and off they went on their honeymoon to live happily ever after. Shortly after they arrived in Italy, Grace contracted a very severe case of chicken pox. She had to be isolated in the hospital, and David eventually had to go back to England. She couldn't speak Italian; the medical staff couldn't speak English.

Nobody knew how deeply this traumatic experience had affected Grace until, shortly after she returned to England, she began to suffer from agoraphobia. Her fear of the outside world was overwhelming and she basically became a recluse.

After considerable help and treatment, she finally dared to open the front door and sweep the steps. But the emotional drain was so much that she had to go back inside; she just couldn't cope.

Eventually she improved and wrote a book about her experiences. This was a rather brave thing to do because she and her husband were extremely well known—he was by then the Bishop of Liverpool. She wrote, "Fear is not only a human response that we all share as human beings but an essential one that needs recognizing, accepting, and managing. Effectively managed, fear ceases to control our actions. Unacknowledged, fear takes control and we find ourselves caught up in varying degrees of destructive behavior."

Recognizing the Fearful Heart

The author of Psalm 27 knew about fear and how to conquer it. Hear his ringing declaration:

> ¹The LORD is my light and my salvation—
>   whom shall I fear?
> The LORD is the stronghold of my life—
>   of whom shall I be afraid?
> ²When evil men advance against me
>   to devour my flesh,
> when my enemies and my foes attack me,
>   they will stumble and fall.
> ³Though an army besiege me,
>   my heart will not fear;
> though war break out against me,
>   even then will I be confident. . . .
>
> ⁵For in the day of trouble
>   he will keep me safe in his dwelling;
> he will hide me in the shelter of his tabernacle
>   and set me high upon a rock.

⁶Then my head will be exalted
   above the enemies who surround me;
 at his tabernacle will I sacrifice with shouts of joy;
   I will sing and make music to the LORD.

Like the psalmist, we need to recognize and accept the fearful parts of our hearts. All human beings experience fear in varying degrees. Fear sometimes has natural causes: we can go through terrifying physical experiences, and they will have a profound effect upon us. We are all familiar with the emotional fallout of people who have gone through the physical horrors of war, suffering that continues even decades after the events.

At other times, fear has psychological causes. Memories of traumatic experiences of childhood can affect us far into adulthood. One time I was jogging with my daughter, Judy. A woman signaled us to stop, which we did. We talked with her briefly but didn't really notice her dog, until for no apparent reason it suddenly bit Judy. As a result of that experience, Judy now has an inordinate fear of dogs when she's running. And I have run hundreds of extra miles simply to avoid the dogs that she refused to pass.

Spiritual causes also contribute to fear. Some people are not sure if they want to believe there is a God to whom they are ultimately accountable, but deep down they really do believe it. When they think of the life that they have lived, of the things that they have done, of actually having to stand before God and give an account for their life, there is an inordinate fear of eternity. This often leads to a fear of dying, which can be related to inordinate fears of illness.

We must come to terms with fear, whatever the causes. As Grace Sheppard reminded us, if we do not manage our fears, they will manage us. Are you facing up to the fears in your life?

Accepting the Fearful Heart

It's one thing to recognize fear and quite another thing to accept it. In his book *Reflections,* the great Swiss physician and counselor Paul Tournier observes, "Fear within certain limits is an eminently useful emotion." There are beneficial aspects of fear when it serves as a means of protection and motivation.

For example, many young mothers today are very fearful of their children being kidnapped. As a result, they exercise tremendous care whenever they take their children out in public. Many good things are done simply because people are motivated by fear. The adrenaline starts pumping, and we discover that we are capable of doing things that we never for a fraction of a moment thought we would ever be able to do.

Let me give you a personal example. The small town in the northwest of England where I grew up was famous for its iron ore. But eventually the mines expired and became derelict. It was a dangerous area because there were all kinds of pits hidden by overgrown brambles, and we boys weren't allowed to go there. But in the autumn, there were magnificent crops of blackberries in this area—a temptation I and my friends couldn't resist.

On one occasion Mr. Redhead, the gamekeeper, surprised a group of us stealing blueberries and began to chase us. Have you ever tried to run along rusty old railroad tracks through disused iron ore mines? It's a bit precarious. The old man was yelling and coming after us, but my younger brother did the most remarkable thing. He absolutely flew past us as if we were going backwards. Fear produced the motivation and the adrenaline, with beneficial effects: we escaped the gamekeeper.

Fear unmanaged, however, can produce all kinds of debilitating effects on how we face the future, the past, and even our present lives. How many people live with great fear in their lives because of the uncertainty of the future? How many children go to bed at night fearful that their parents might get divorced? How many men go to bed at night worrying whether or not they'll have a job in the morning? How many people worry if they can pay the bills if they ever get sick?

Fear about the future.

Concern for the future can be so debilitating for some people that it almost paralyzes them. As a result, they look for all kinds of security. Sometimes so great is the uncertainty, so deep-rooted is the fear that they look for security in situations and relationships that in actual fact are going to exacerbate the problem. If fear of the future is not managed properly, it can lead us into destructive behaviors.

Many people try to find relief from the uncertainties of the future through what I call escapist lifestyles. Rather than confront the future, they seek ways of filling up the present, often with increasingly bizarre escapades and habits. Drinking, casual sex, and drug experimentation are some of the risky behaviors that can have serious repercussions. The fear of the uncertainty of the future is often increased by the way people handle that fear.

Fear about the past.

It's not just the future but the past that often brings haunting fear with it. Some people feel desperately guilty about their past. Many would hate for their spouses to know what they have done in the past. Other people would hate for their spouses to know what they're doing right now. Some people who have cheated in one way or another are desperately afraid that the IRS will actually catch up to them. Other folks have so much garbage swept under the rug that they live with an inordinate sense of culpability and don't know how to cope with it. So they live a life of dissembling, lying, cheating, and covering up.

Fear about the present.
Many people have an overwhelming sense of inadequacy concerning the present. They are in circumstances they just can't handle, and they either find themselves passively drifting into depression or aggressively becoming angry. If the anger isn't carefully handled, it could degenerate into acts of violence.

You know as well as I do that all these feelings and responses are going on in our culture. But have you ever thought about how these reactions are directly or indirectly related to fear? Fortunately, the Scriptures have something to tell us on the subject.

Managing the Fearful Heart

One way the psalmist manages his fearful heart is by making sure that he has the correct perspective. Psalm 27:1 says "The LORD is my light and my salvation." This is a theological statement. As a result of that affirmation, he then asks a practical rhetorical question: "Whom shall I fear?" The practical realities of the psalmist's life are rooted in theological conviction. As if to press the point home, he continues, "The LORD is the stronghold of my life." He mentions the immediate fearful circumstances of his life in verse 2, but then comes out with the great statement: "Though an army besiege me, my heart will not fear" (vs. 3).

One step in managing fear is to keep perspective by starting with the Lord, the One who shines light into the dark, uncertain areas of life. God shines the light of his truth into the darkness of our fearful confusion. We discover that the fears we are experiencing because of uncertainty of the future begin to dissipate as the Lord becomes our light and shines his truth on our circumstances. We can then begin to say, at the risk of giving way to a cliché, "I don't know what the future holds, but I do know the One who holds my future." The emphasis, the perspective, the focus is on the Lord, who is my light.

The phrase "The Lord is . . . my salvation" can be interpreted and applied in different ways, for there are so many things from which we need to be saved. We need to be saved from our past. We need to be saved from the consequences of the things we did in the past. We need to be saved from the consequences of the things that we should have done in the past and didn't do. But how do any of us adequately deal with our past?

All of my past actions have gone into eternity before the eyes of an eternal God. As far as I am concerned, the past is past; as far as he's concerned, it is eternally present. If anything is to be done about my past, only God can do it. The Lord is my salvation, who is graciously prepared to forgive. He takes away the fear that comes from culpability concerning the past.

But there remains a problem between our past and our future. We live in the present. But hear this: The Lord is the stronghold of our lives in *all* the day-to-day experiences, past, present, and future. As the psalmist states in Psalm 23, "Surely goodness and love will follow me *all the days of my life*" (italics mine). God is the One to whom we can turn. He is the One in whom we can trust. He is the One who is bigger than the things that have caused the doubt of fear to spring deep into our hearts.

As you recognize and accept the fears in your life, as you realize the way in which some fears can have a positive impact and how other fears can become debilitating, to whom or what do you turn? Is it to a Lord whom you know as your light and salvation, the stronghold of your life? This clearly is the situation of the psalmist as he translates and applies his understanding of the Lord to specific areas of fear-inducing circumstances.

A Matter of Priority

You have heard stories of people who find a magic lantern, and after rubbing it a genie appears and grants them one wish. In the same way, picture the Lord tapping you on the shoulder at a moment of deep devotion and meditation and saying, "Ask me one thing—any one thing." I wonder what it would be. The psalmist here, generally assumed to be David, talks about the one request he makes of the Lord:

> 4One thing I ask of the LORD,
>   this is what I seek:
> that I may dwell in the house of the LORD
>   all the days of my life,
> to gaze upon the beauty of the LORD
>   and to seek him in his temple.

How impractical this wish may seem. But it is only as he focuses on who the Lord is that he can begin to be capable of living in the midst of a fear-inducing situation.

Someone very close to me, who shall be nameless, loses her keys regularly. Whenever this person loses keys, this person prays about it. I have never made any claim to be anywhere as spiritual as this person, so I actually look for them. This person asks; I seek. We've been quite a formidable team, lo these many years.

Usually as I look for the lost keys, I go about it logically, seek carefully, and leave no stone unturned. When I eventually do find the keys, this colleague of mine praises God and says, "What an answer to prayer." Are we supposed to ask, or are we supposed to seek? The answer is yes and yes. The priority in dealing with all the fear-inducing aspects of life is to be with God, to focus on who he is. He is our only hope, and we need to get to know him better by asking for this and by seeking him.

Remember that David was a soldier. Theologians tell us that in all probability this psalm was written around the time he was going to go off to war again—a fear-inducing situation if ever there was one. He is saying in effect, "If there's one thing I could really ask of the Lord, it would be that I could quit being a soldier and just sit around the temple all day long. That's what I'd really like to do." Of course, in a literal, practical sense, that is not what he is going to be allowed to do.

But in a spiritual sense, he's really saying, "In my circumstances, whatever they are, I understand the one priority must be this—that I might deepen my knowledge of God, that I might gaze upon his beauty as I seek him in his temple. I'm going to ask the Lord for this and take the practical steps to see the prayer answered. And when I do that, in the day of trouble he will keep me safe." Many people do not get the perspective and the priority right, so the day of trouble overwhelms them. They begin to scramble for answers, their fear is never dealt with, and they often end up in self-destructive behaviors and relationships.

The Beauty of the Lord

Let's be practical for a minute. If David had gone to the temple—actually the tabernacle at that time—what would he have seen? He would have seen the area called the Holy of Holies where God dwelt, but he would not be allowed to enter there because of the great, impenetrable veil. Even if he had gone in, it would have been completely dark. So how in the world could he "see" the beauty of the Lord there? He would have been allowed to enter the outer court, where he would have seen priests bustling around and farmers bringing sheep, goats, and bulls that were then slaughtered for sacrifices. Would that be "seeing the beauty of the Lord"?

The beauty and goodness of the Lord is seen first of all in the fact that he is the holiest of holy, that he is utterly separate, that a mere mortal cannot move into his presence. He is so holy, pure, and separate from our sin that we would shrivel in his presence. There is an impenetrableness about God. He transcends all things. He is high and holy and awesome. I believe that one of the great needs in our contemporary culture is for people to see these attributes of God in all his transcendent sovereign majesty. When fears overwhelm you, you don't need a buddy; you need an awesome, holy, sovereign, majestic, omnipotent God.

If David had seen the Holy of Holies where God dwelt in the tabernacle, it would have been awe-inspiring but also discouraging. But he had looked at the sacrificial system of worship and heard the ancient words that came from God, "It is the blood that makes atonement for one's life" (Lev. 17:11), and "without the shedding of blood there is no forgiveness" (Heb. 9:22). The beauty of God's forgiving Spirit and the wonder of knowing peace with God thrilled David's heart.

We look on the beauty of our God, and what do we see? On the one hand, his holy, magnificent, awe-inspiring, sovereign, omnipotent majesty; on the other hand, his incredible grace, his majestic mercy, his reaching out to us. We have no right to enter into his presence. We have only the opportunity of coming humbly before him and casting our puniness on his omnipotence, our weakness on his strength, our sinfulness on his grace, our failure on his mercy, and trusting him.

Practice Makes Patience

Finally, the psalmist points out his firm persuasion:

> 13I am still confident of this:
>   I will see the goodness of the LORD
>   in the land of the living.
> 14Wait for the LORD;
>   be strong and take heart
>   and wait for the LORD.

As David marches off into battle with fearful situations to the left and to the right, before him and behind him, how can he be confident? He has rolled the burden upon an omnipotent, gracious, and merciful God, who not only has become his light and his salvation but is also the stronghold of his life. Believing these things, "whom shall I fear?" is the natural response.

But his persuasion becomes a matter of practice as well. Verse 14 counsels, "Wait for the LORD; be strong and take heart and wait for the LORD." To wait for the Lord, in very practical terms, means to be *patient*. God moves at his own speed, not ours. We are desperately impatient; he inhabits eternity.

Waiting for the Lord also means to be *expectant*. Say a man arranges to meet his date at a certain place at a certain time. She is late. He is patient, but he is also expectant. He looks for the moment when she'll come around the corner, and . . . there she is! It was worth the wait. It was worth being patient, and his expectancy paid off.

Oh, that we might move into a relationship with the Lord where we may gaze upon his beauty, where we may seek him, and where we may understand him in all his glory. Then we could translate the truth of who he is into our life situations and in the day of trouble, we would not be fearful.

Surrendering Our Fear

What do you fear most? Are you managing it or is it managing you? Is the thing you fear smaller or bigger than your God? How well do you know him? Can you bring it to him and say, "The LORD is my light and my salvation—whom shall I fear? The LORD is the stronghold of my life—of whom shall I be afraid"?

The apostle Paul puts this truth rather differently but very powerfully: "Who shall separate us from the love of Christ? Shall trouble or hardship or persecution or famine or nakedness or danger or sword?" (Rom. 8:35). He was not dreaming up weird things to be fearful about. He was simply cataloguing the things he had gone through on a regular basis. "No," he affirms. "In all these things we are more than conquerors through him who loved us. For I am convinced that neither death nor life, neither angels nor demons, neither the present nor the future, nor any powers, neither height nor depth, nor anything else in all creation, will be able to separate us from the love of God that is in Christ Jesus our Lord" (Rom. 8:37-39).

The apostle John adds this thought to the topic at hand, "Perfect love drives out fear" (1 John 4:18). From whence comes this perfect love? From the God we know who, in Christ, has given himself for our redemption, so that we can say with the psalmist, "He is my light. He is my salvation. He is the stronghold of my life. Whom shall I fear? Though an enemy encamp against me, I will not be afraid." Jesus put it this way: "Do not be afraid of those who kill the body but cannot kill the soul. Rather, be afraid of the One who can destroy both soul and body in hell" (Matt. 10:28). Make sure that you can fear the Lord, and then you have nothing else to fear.

All of us have our own particular fears, anxieties, and worries. Some of us are fearful because we recognize that life is beyond our control. Others are fearful of what might happen or what people might do to us. Some are afraid of what God might do to us. God knows what is going on in your heart. Trust him to help you recognize and manage your fears. If your grasp on God is tenuous today, ask him by his gracious Spirit to spark within you a desire to know him and to deal with your fearful heart.

6

The Frustrated Heart

Psalm 37

"Image is everything" our culture screams at us. Dress for success. Convey a good impression. Get the perfect relationship or job. These outward aspects of life are what human beings are often most interested in. As we have seen, the Bible reminds us that God is more interested in the heart than in the externals. It is out of the heart that the issues of life come. Is it any wonder that the Bible mentions the *heart* almost a thousand times?

Psalm 37 is another well-known passage of Scripture attributed to David. It speaks of human desire as well as the all-too-human tendency to look at what others have rather than looking to God. In this chapter we will look at the longings of the human heart, the frustrations our unmet desires can bring, and how our desires can square with God's priorities.

Let's look at the first part of Psalm 37:

¹Do not fret because of evil men
    or be envious of those who do wrong;
²for like the grass they will soon wither,
    like green plants they will soon die away.

³Trust in the LORD and do good;
    dwell in the land and enjoy safe pasture.
⁴Delight yourself in the LORD
    and he will give you the desires of your heart.

⁵Commit you way to the LORD;
    trust in him and he will do this:
⁶He will make your righteousness shine like the
        dawn,
    the justice of your cause like the noonday sun.

⁷Be still before the LORD and wait patiently for him;
    do not fret when men succeed in their ways,
    when they carry out their wicked schemes.

⁸Refrain from anger and turn from wrath;
    do not fret—it leads only to evil.
⁹For evil men will be cut off,
    but those who hope in the LORD will inherit the
        land.

¹⁰A little while, and the wicked will be no more;
    though you look for them, they will not be
        found.
¹¹But the meek will inherit the land
    and enjoy great peace.

The Frustration of Unfulfilled Desires

It's a good rule of biblical interpretation that if you find a phrase repeated in a context, in all probability that's what the context is about. Three times in this psalm we read the command "Do not fret." *Fret* is not a word we use frequently today. "Don't get frustrated" would perhaps be more relevant to us.

But life *is* frustrating. Many people have deep longings and aspirations in their hearts, but circumstances are such that they don't come to fruition. Frustration often follows. The psalmist, however, tells us that we've got to be able to handle life's frustrations even though our longing hearts may not find satisfaction. Why do we find so often that our longings are not met? Why is it that so often unfulfilled desires become the dominant theme of our existence?

Young couples marry and look forward to children, and then they confront infertility. A woman is doing well in her job and then—without any warning—she is laid off. She tries earnestly to find other work, but the offers don't come. A single man has a real desire to be married, but serious dating relationships are few and far between. The frustrations build. What are we to do with all these unfulfilled desires?

"Delight yourself in the LORD and he will give you the desires of your heart," says Psalm 37:4. We've got a problem here. We know we're supposed to believe verses like this. We've got them underlined in our Bibles until the ink bleeds through to the maps. But many of us, if we are honest, would say that behind our smiling exterior is a heart that's frustrated because of unfulfilled desires. Why does Scripture make such a promise if our desires are unfulfilled?

The psalm encourages us, "Commit your way to the LORD; trust in him and he will do this: He will make your righteousness shine like the dawn, the justice of your cause like the noonday sun" (vss. 5-6). In short, he will give you the desires of your heart. Now, this does not mean you can come before God with any old thing on your mind and say, "Oh, God, you said it. I believe it. That settles it. I desire this. Do it!"

No, it has to do with your righteousness shining like

the dawn and the justice of your cause like the noonday sun. In other words, the desires of your heart have to be legitimate. They have to be right. They have to be in accordance with the eternal purposes of God, who wills what is best for you, not just what you want.

An example of questionable desires comes from the early days of Billy Graham's ministry in England. I remember that he was something of a phenomenon there. This long, lanky fellow wore flashy ties the like of which we'd never seen before and spoke with his very appealing North Carolinian drawl. He was somewhat different from our normal English clergymen, to put it mildly. At that time the beautiful young actress Elizabeth Taylor was hitting the headlines, but she had some health problems. Graham told a congregation to which he was preaching, "Don't envy Elizabeth Taylor. Pray for her." A man in the back row stood up and said, "I pray for her every night, but I never get her." I wonder if he had underlined Psalm 37:4 in his Bible?

A young soldier was desperately injured in the Civil War and crippled for the rest of his life. Reflecting on his life and his heart's desires, this is what he wrote:

> I asked for strength that I might achieve.
> I was made weak that I might obey.
> I asked for health that I might do greater things.
> I was given infirmity that I might do better things.
> I asked for riches that I might be happy.
> I was given poverty that I might be wise.
> I asked for power that I might have the praise of
>   men.
> I was given weaknesses that I might feel the need
>   of God.
> I asked for all things that I might enjoy life.
> I was given life that I might enjoy all things.
> I have received nothing I asked for and all that I
>   hoped for.
> My prayer is answered.

A similar perspective was shared by Joachim Neander, a German pastor. He was thirty years old and dying of tuberculosis when he wrote one of the great hymns of the faith, "Praise to the Lord, the Almighty."

Praise to the Lord,
    who o'er all things so wondrously reigneth,
Shelters thee under His wings,
    yea, so gently sustaineth!
Hast thou not seen
    all that is needful hath been
Granted in what he ordaineth?

What a comfort! God gives what he ordains, knowing his will will truly satisfy us. If God really gave us *all* the things we desire, there would be such an illegitimacy to them that they would be desperately detrimental to us. But one thing we can be convinced of in the area of the unfulfilled desires: if we are bringing our longings before God according to his righteousness and according to his sovereign purposes, he is committed to granting to us that which is best for his purposes. Though it can be frustrating to wait, we will receive what is best for us in the long run.

Why Do They Have It So Good?

The psalmist also addresses the frustration of life's injustices. He seems to be really rankled by the inequities of life. One of the biggest injustices that Christians discover is that being a believer can be so hard while unbelievers seem to have it so easy. If *we* were God, we'd probably reorganize it: "Okay believers, you're the good kids on the block. You can have it real good, and I'll zap these other guys. I'll show them." For some reason, it doesn't seem to work that way. The ungodly seem to have it so good and enjoy the enviable things.

If you leaf through popular magazines today, you can

read about the rich and the famous. You'll see all the stuff that they're enjoying, all the stuff you'd really like to enjoy, all the stuff that once in a while you feel envious about. If only I could have that or do that, you think. It's not fair.

But the psalmist urges us: "Do not fret because of evil men or be envious of those who do wrong. . . . Be still before the LORD and wait patiently for him; do not fret when men succeed in their ways, when they carry out their wicked schemes" (vss. 1, 7). Our hearts cry out, "God, do you know that many of these successful people are really rascals? Do you know that the man who works in the office next to me is cutting all the corners and padding his expense report? Do you know, God, that I am the straight arrow and would you believe he gets the sales awards? Are you listening, God?"

The ungodly seem to get away with murder, as verse 12 hints: "The wicked plot against the righteous and gnash their teeth at them." In situations when we try to do what's right, we just get gnashed on by these people. The unbelievers get away with it. Verses 16 and 17 say, "Better the little that the righteous have than the wealth of many wicked; for the power of the wicked will be broken, but the LORD upholds the righteous." Yeah, right, you say. That's good. But notice that it's the wicked who have the wealth and it's the wicked who have the power. Why is it, Lord, that these people who have it all are the ones who don't do it the way you say it should be done? It's not right. It's not fair. It's a very frustrating business seeing the way the ungodly have it so good.

Verse 21 says bluntly, "The wicked borrow and do not repay." They get away with dishonesty. It's amazing how some folk can go on serenely from one scam to another scheme and another scam, and they never get caught. They just get all the breaks. And as if that isn't enough, the psalmist recounts, "I have seen a wicked and ruthless man flourishing like a green tree in its native soil" (vs. 35). Life is unjust. Not only do the ungodly seem to have it so good, but the godly often find life so difficult. They're required to trust God when they don't understand.

Hard to Trust

Some may ask, Why do we have to trust God when other people aren't trusting God and life seems to work out for them? Sometimes it sounds appealing to just do life on our own. We'd rather plan the whole thing, try to control the whole thing. That's what the wicked are doing, and it seems to work. It's hard to trust God when life is not fair.

In verse 7 we read, "Be still before the LORD and wait patiently for him." But Lord, you say, unbelievers don't wait patiently for anybody, why do I have to wait patiently? Why doesn't God just do something? It's very difficult being patient when nobody else is.

Again the Lord urges us in the psalm, "Refrain from anger and turn from wrath" (vs. 8). There you go again, Lord. Now I've got to keep my cool when nobody else does. It would be so nice if just once in a while you'd give me a day off. Say I'm in the airport and my flight is canceled. I watch everybody else lose their cool, bang on the desk, demand this, demand the other, and very quickly get help. Then I come up all quiet and gracious and no one takes any notice of me. Lord, what I'd really like to do is just let 'er rip like everybody else. Why do I have to refrain from anger and turn from wrath? It's very hard to do good when other people won't.

On top of everything, I'm supposed to be generous. You admit, Lord, that it's "better the little that the righteous have than the wealth of many wicked" (vs. 16). Let me get all this straight, God. You say that if I do things your way, I probably won't have as much as the wicked but I've got to share my little, and that the wicked who have a lot won't share what they've got. Now that's not fair. It's very hard to give generously when others don't.

God says that believers are the ones who have to be

generous when other people aren't. We are the ones who have to be meek when other people rip us off. We are the ones who need to keep our cool when others lose their temper. We are the ones who still wait while others pass us by. God wants us to trust him, rather than safely organize and control our lives.

Is your heart frustrated? My heart often is. Life is filled with the frustrations of unfulfilled desires, the frustrations of life's injustices, and the frustrations of life's battles. Psalm 37 is very straightforward about this. In verses 23 and 24 David talks about the struggles that we have against life's stumbling blocks. Verses 31 and 32 remind us that life is full of slippery slopes and hidden pitfalls. Life is full of battles. Even though in our hearts these frustrations are building up, we can't get around how we are called to respond: "Trust in the LORD and do good. . . . Delight yourself in the LORD, . . . Commit your way to the LORD; trust in him."

Truth for the Frustrated Heart

What does all this mean? Four truths come through loudly and clearly in this psalm:

- ❑ Good will eventually prevail (vss. 9-15).
- ❑ God will eternally triumph (vss. 18-20).
- ❑ Grace will continually flow (vss. 23-25).
- ❑ Godliness will ultimately satisfy (vss. 37-40).

Do we honestly believe that good will eventually prevail? All around us we see people who are not interested in doing good but who are apparently succeeding very nicely. Over and over again in this psalm we are told not to get worked up or frustrated because of all these people, "For evil men will be cut off" (vs. 9); "A little while, and the wicked will be no more" (vs. 10); "the LORD laughs at the wicked, for he knows their day is coming" (vs. 13).

Are we convinced that God will eternally triumph? Do we know the end of the story? Do we know that, for reasons known only to himself, God is at work even in circumstances like this? The psalmist gives us some perspective:

18The days of the blameless are known
   to the LORD,
      and their inheritance will endure forever.
19In times of disaster they will not wither;
      in days of famine they will enjoy plenty.

20But the wicked will perish:
   The LORD's enemies will be like the beauty of
      the fields,
      they will vanish—vanish like smoke.

Are we certain that grace will continually flow in hard situations? We are in such a "fix-it" frame of mind in this culture. We assume that we have the right to get a cure for everything as quickly, as painlessly, and as inexpensively as possible, even though reality tells us that there are some things for which there are no solutions, there are some things that are not going to get fixed, there are some things that will only be fixed very slowly. Verses 23-25 promise that even in chronically difficult situations, God will be faithful:

23If the LORD delights in a man's way,
      he makes his steps firm;
24though he stumble, he will not fall,
      for the LORD upholds him with his hand.

25I was young and now I am old,
      yet I have never seen the righteous forsaken
      or their children begging bread.

Do we live as if godliness will ultimately satisfy? The psalmist believed this was true. He closes with these words:

[37]Consider the blameless, observe the upright;
   there is a future for the man of peace.
[38] But all sinners will be destroyed;
   the future of the wicked will be cut off.

[39]The salvation of the righteous comes from the LORD;
   he is their stronghold in time of trouble.
[40]The LORD helps them and delivers them;
   he delivers them from the wicked and saves them,
   because they take refuge in him.

There are times when godliness becomes a burden, when struggling against selfishness becomes onerous, when living righteously is costly. To make matters worse, the ungodly live in casual carelessness, and godlessness wears the seductive garb of supposed joyous living. At such times God's people must challenge their own heart's devotion and review their convictions. They must remind themselves that godliness is the *right* way to live, with its own temporal and eternal rewards.

God will not forsake us. Godly living is ultimately the best way to go. Will you allow the frustrations of life to govern your heart? Or will you allow these four fundamental principles to be the bedrock of your life and the cause of your joyful attitudes?

Peace for the Longing Heart

If it is true that these four principles apply in frustrating circumstances, then three simple disciplines of life are necessary to put them into action.

1. Trust God and do good.

Are you trusting God to deal with all your past, all the pasts with all its shame, all the pasts with all the stuff you don't want to be written about, all the pasts that you can't forgive yourself for? Are you trusting God for Christ's sake to forgive that? If God is trustworthy enough to deal with your past and with your future, what suddenly went wrong with God that you can't trust him today? Trusting him frees us to obey him and act rightly.

Viktor Frankl survived a Nazi concentration camp, where he observed that, when people were starving because there wasn't enough bread to go around, some actually shared their meager rations with more needy people. He learned that, even in the most horrific situations where people seem totally controlled, there is one thing still in their control: they can still do what's right.

2. Delight yourself so much in the Lord that he'll give you a new set of desires.

Take delight in the Lord, understanding that he then will begin to work on changing your desires and fulfilling your longings. Then you won't be demanding your own meager desires but will be open and ready for his greater good for you.

How, you may ask, do I "delight in the Lord"? The same way you delight in a new baby's gurgle, a cardinal's full-throated song at dawn, the whisper of the breeze in the rushes by a pond. You allow your mind to absorb the details, your emotions to respond to the stimulus of what you observe, and then find ways of expressing your joy.

3. Commit your way to the Lord and trust in him.

Notice that it is necessary to do the initial committing and the continual trusting. I well remember a particularly hair-raising experience when the welcoming committee who greeted me at the airport led me to a car in which we drove off at a furious rate. The driver was so busy turning her head to talk to me in the back seat that she ran a stop sign. Noticing my detachment, she complained, "I do believe you're not listening, Mr. Briscoe." I replied, "I'm afraid I wasn't. I was watching the road."

My problem was that after I had originally committed

myself to the car, I couldn't go on trusting in the driver! Not so with God. Our initial commitment, and his faithfulness, should lead to increasing trust.

God knows how frustrating it is down here. He knows how hard it is to see evil seem to win and good people of faith suffer. He knows our deepest longings. You must trust him, and he in turn will work on your desires and touch you in such a way that you're no longer a frustrated victim of your circumstances. Instead, you will be a person with a peace that passes understanding deep in your heart.

7

The Angry Heart

Psalm 39

Since "no-fault divorce" became the law of the land, countless people have suffered the indignity of being hauled into court. There they have been told their marriage no longer exists and half of their assets have been taken from them. They have listened to total strangers, attorneys, and judges discuss and decide the future of their children. It is hard to imagine a situation more designed to create frustration, resentment, anger, despair, and anxiety.

When traumatic or unexpected events like divorce come our way, we often feel so utterly helpless. There's nothing we can do about them. Life is like that, introducing us to difficult circumstances or people about which or about whom we can do nothing at all.

Human beings love to think that we are in control of our lives. But when we lose control, anxiety results. Anxiety can turn into resentment. Resentment can become anger. Psalm 39 shows us that if these emotions are not handled well, we may experience all kinds of negative effects in our lives—physiological, psychological, relational, and spiritual.

Something traumatic happened to the writer of Psalm 39. We don't know what it was, and that's probably just as well. If the psalmist had outlined for us specifically what happened to him, there's always the possibility that we would say, "Oh, well, that's nothing. You should see what happened to me." But because we don't know what his particular problem was, we can all relate to and learn from his response and feelings.

How Do You Handle Anger?

Before we look at the passage, I'd like to discuss this topic of anger. When it comes to anger—an indignant reaction to a real or perceived injustice—there are different ways that we can handle it. Four classic ways are repression, suppression, expression, and confession.

Repression

When we talk about repression, we mean that we are angry but we refuse to admit it. We have been exposed to somebody or something that has imposed upon us that which is unjust. We feel that we have been demeaned. We feel that we have not been treated in an appropriate manner. We may call it something else, but we refuse to acknowledge, even to ourselves, that anger is underneath.

This is not an uncommon approach among evangelical Christians. Many believers have the idea that anger, by definition, is always wrong. They feel that the way to handle it is simply to deny that it's there, and then to behave in such a manner that they do not convey any angry feelings.

Of course, this is based on erroneous thinking because anger is not always wrong. God is good, holy, and sometimes angry. God would not be God if he were not angry at times. If God was not indignant at injustice and evil, then he would fail to be a just and righteous God. Human beings at times are required to be good and angry. Therefore we should not assume that anger is always wrong, and we should never fall into the trap of feeling that repressing and hiding anger is the way to handle it.

A woman called me on one occasion, and I answered the phone, "Hello, Stuart Briscoe here."

She began with, "Now, Stuart, I don't want you to think I'm angry."

"Why then did you bring up the subject?" I replied.

And she promptly exploded. She was in classic repression of anger, madder than a wet hornet but not prepared to admit it, especially to herself.

Suppression

Suppressing anger means that when we are indignant about a particular situation or person, we feel that we must not in any way let other people know that we're angry. Therefore, rather than expressing it, we push it it all down inside.

Imagine for a moment that you are in a committee meeting of some sort. You make a proposal but nobody takes it seriously. You can't even get a second for the motion. You feel totally demeaned and overlooked. But you know that you can't in any way let the people know. You mustn't "be angry" about it. So you sit quietly and get very cool, then cold, then withdrawn, and then bitter. Perhaps you have nothing to do with those people ever again. You pride yourself that you never "got angry," when in actual fact you were as angry as it was possible to be. You simply suppressed it.

The main problem, of course, with repressing or suppressing anger is that if these emotions are not dealt with they will become, as the psalmist put it, like a fire inside you, stoking up like the molten core inside of the earth which eventually bursts out through a weak spot in a volcanic eruption. Denied anger can burst out eventually in inappropriate, abusive, or even violent behavior.

Expression

Then there are other people who pride themselves that they never hide their feelings: "You never need to worry what I'm thinking; I'll let you know. You'll know how I feel about every situation." For some strange reason, these people feel that, when they are angry, it is appropriate that they exhibit absolutely no self-control and let it all hang out.

Some have even learned a Greek word to explain and excuse their behavior: *katharsis,* from which our word "catharsis" comes, which means a purification or purgation of the emotions (such as pity or fear). They talk knowledgeably about how expressing their feelings and getting all the junk out is cathartic. They may feel better not bottling it up, but everyone else suffers because the junk has exploded all over them.

Confession

There is another way to approach anger: confess it. Confession works on a simple, basic premise: There is a God who made us, through whom and for whom we live, and unto whom we are accountable. It stands to reason that if we are in a relationship with this God, then all the circumstances of our lives that cause anger are relevant, as far as he is concerned. Moreover, we cannot possibly handle these situations without relating them to God.

It never occurs to some people that they need to be seeing their anger-inducing circumstances in terms of the God from whom they come and to whom they go. They simply respond on an earthly level with little or no concept of the eternal, divine perspective. To handle anger properly requires appropriate confession in the heavenly dimension. This means I come before the Lord and talk about the circumstances, the trauma, the hurt, my reactions, and begin to be honest with God about my feelings. Then and only then will I be in a position rightly to handle confession in the other earthly dimension by talking to the people concerned.

Sometimes when we're angry with people, we will talk to them all right—red in the face, perspiring heavily, with our finger pointing at them. That is an inappropriate way of doing it. Always remember that when you point a finger at somebody there are three fingers pointing back at you—a silent reminder to be careful what you are saying. When you handle anger by saying "You did this" and "You did that," you create a barrier. You'll find yourself in an adversarial position. And I promise you that the situation will be "improved" a hundred times worse.

Alternatively, having confessed your anger to the Lord, received his perspective on the whole thing, and found his grace to handle the situation, then you can go to the person concerned. Instead of predicating everything on "you," you base it on "I." Instead of the pointed finger, use the hand on the chest. "I have a concern. I may be misunderstanding this. I need to tell you what I'm feeling about this." A bridge may be built, and you're more likely to receive an empathetic response.

The Angry Psalmist

Let's turn now to Psalm 39 and note how the psalmist responded to his traumatic event. In the first three verses we read:

> [1]I said, "I will watch my ways
>   and keep my tongue from sin;
> I will put a muzzle on my mouth
>   as long as the wicked are in my presence."
> [2]But when I was silent and still,
>   not even saying anything good,
>   my anguish increased.
> [3]My heart grew hot within me,
>   and as I meditated, the fire burned;
>   then I spoke with my tongue.

Was the psalmist in repression? Was he refusing to admit that he was angry? No. Was he in expression? Was he letting it all hang out? No. Was he in confession in the early part of it? No, he wasn't. What was he doing? He put a muzzle on his mouth; he was suppressing his anger.

Let's look very carefully at these three verses because there's much that will be helpful to us in them. Notice, first of all, his hasty reaction to these traumatic circumstances. He decided, "I am in an anger-inducing situation. I fully realize that I could do some very bad things at this particular time under these circumstances. Not only that, I fully recognize that I could say some things out of my anger at this time which will exacerbate the problem. Therefore, I will make a decision. In the heat of the moment I will watch my step and I will muzzle my mouth because I can make things a hundred times worse if I don't."

The psalmist was also very conscious of the fact that he was surrounded by ungodly people: "I will watch my ways . . . as long as the wicked are in my presence." Perhaps he mused, "I have a responsibility to these ungodly people. And if I react to my traumatic circumstances as *they* usually do, then how can I ever expect to have any credibility with them?" With this in mind, he wanted to keep his "tongue from sin."

Why would the ungodly think that godliness pays dividends if, in traumatic circumstances, we behave no differently from the ungodly? What if we're just as objectionable, crabby, angry, mean, or self-centered? What if we drive or push into line the same way everybody else does? So we applaud the psalmist. He's made a commendable decision to not say anything bad out of a genuine concern.

However, I believe he took this response to a misguided extreme. He acknowledged, "When I was silent and still, not even saying anything good, my anguish increased. My heart grew hot within me, and as I meditated, the fire burned" (vss. 2-3). No explosion here. No sense that he is going to let it all hang out. No refusal here. But when he decided he would not say anything bad, he also decided that he would not say anything good either. In other words, "I'm not going to say anything, period." He clamped down and clammed up. He became removed and remote.

If he's not going to say *anything,* how in the world is the psalmist going to have the fellowship that is so necessary to live as a godly person? One cannot be a disciple in isolation. What's more, if he's not going to say anything good, then praise and worship are ruled out when he is angry. So he becomes ingrown, inward-looking, absorbed with his situation. He says nothing good, and he says nothing bad.

As a result, we find something that is highly predictable. Notice what he says in verse 3: "My heart grew hot within me, and as I meditated, the fire burned." Don't be misled by that word *meditated.* Usually when we read it in the Bible we assume it means meditating on the things of God, some sort of devotional experience. But that's not what the psalmist is talking about here. He is meditating upon what led him to be angry.

My wife, Jill, met a woman who told her with great distress and anguish about her abusive marriage. It obviously was highly traumatic for her. But as Jill listened, something didn't quite ring true. So she asked the woman, "When did this abusive behavior last happen?"

The woman replied, "Oh, we were divorced fifteen years ago."

"You mean the abuse that you're talking about stopped more than fifteen years ago?"

"Oh, yes," she answered.

"Well, it really didn't stop, did it?" Jill responded. "It was going on this morning when you got up. It was going on last night when you went to bed. It was going on a few minutes ago while you talked to me. You're going over and over and over it. You're reliving it and reliving it and reliving it. You're feeding on it, and it's feeding on you."

In a similar way, the psalmist was going over and over and over what made him angry. He was feeding on it and it was feeding on him, and the fire in his soul was being stoked.

A Turning Point

Finally something happens. The psalmist says, "My heart grew hot within me, and as I meditated, the fire burned; *then I spoke with my tongue*" (italics mine). What is he going to say? He's been holding it in so long his heart is like the molten center of the earth. Look out! The volcano is going to burst. Fortunately, though, he doesn't explode. Instead, he says these incredible words:

> 4"Show me, O LORD, my life's end
>   and the number of my days;
>   let me know how fleeting is my life.
> 5You have made my days a mere handbreadth;
>   the span of my years is as nothing before you.
>   Each man's life is but a breath.
> 6Man is a mere phantom as he goes to and fro:
>   He bustles about, but only in vain;
>   he heaps us wealth, not knowing who will get it."

The psalmist takes a cooling-off period, a time-out during which he engages in some honest reflection. Notice the direction of his reflection: he turns to prayer and talks to the Lord. Some may say, "Why would he do that? He's just spiritualizing what is clearly a psychological problem."

I firmly believe that human beings are psychological creatures, but they are primarily spiritual creatures. No solutions arise if the spiritual dimension is divorced from the situation. When trauma occurs, many turn to a counselor. That is most appropriate, but often we look to the counselor to come up with all the solutions. It is not uncommon for us in our psychologically oriented society to look for psychological solutions to all our problems. We must insist on bringing in the divine, eternal dimension to our deliberations. We must come to God in prayer, asking, "Show me, God. I need divine insight into this situation. I need your perspective on this thing. Without it, there is no way that I can understand my humanity or my feelings."

Life Is Short

The psalmist says something very wise to the Lord: "Show me my life's end and the number of my days." I believe the phrase "life's end" here means the purpose of his life. The psalmist is asking, in effect, "Why am I here? If I don't know why I am here, how in the world can I cope with being here? And a major part of coping with being here is coping with these horrible circumstances. Lord, show me my life's purpose. Show me what the point of existence is."

One question in the Westminster Catechism asks, "What is the chief end of man?" The answer: "To glorify God and enjoy him forever." How in the world can we glorify God in traumatic circumstances that are inducing a lot of anger? The only way to glorify God is to obey and trust. So we look at the anger-inducing situations we are in and ask these questions:

❐ In this situation, am I trusting God, or am I looking for all kinds of ways of getting even?

❐ Am I looking for ways of venting my anger and showing everybody that I'm right and everybody else is wrong?

❐ How am I relating to the people concerned? Am I relating in a manner that will glorify God, in dependence upon his Spirit?

The psalmist also asks the Lord to give him insights on the transient nature of his existence. He begins to recognize how incredibly brief life is. My sister-in-law, one of my favorite people, recognizes this perspective. She has a very simple philosophy as a result: *Life is too short to fall out with anybody.* Many people today have a burning heart, fueled by a reserve of anger. They hold onto it as a precious commodity and they justify themselves in it. A trying situation does matter a lot when you're in it. But in the light of eternity, does it really matter all that much?

Three Responses to a Burning Heart

The psalmist is facing an anger-inducing situation. He's tried stuffing it. It doesn't work; the fire burns hotter. In the end he realizes he needs to reflect and come to the Lord in prayer. He needs to confess and gain the divine and eternal perspective. He needs to understand the purpose of existence. He needs to come to terms with his own humanity. If he doesn't, how in the world can he ever handle the situation?

7"But now, Lord, what do I look for?
   My hope is in you.
8Save me from all my transgressions;
   do not make me the scorn of fools.
9I was silent; I would not open my mouth,
   for you are the one who has done this.
10Remove your scourge from me;
   I am overcome by the blow of your hand.
11You rebuke and discipline men for their sin;
   you consume their wealth like a moth—
   each man is but a breath."

The psalmist responds to his situation with a statement, a request, and an acceptance of discipline.

1. A statement of confidence in the Lord.

"My hope is in you." In these traumatic circumstances, in this anger-inducing situation, where does the psalmist's ultimate confidence lie? In the Lord. Were he with us today, he might say, "I'm not going to put all my confidence in the church. I'm not going to put it in the support group. I'm not going to put it in a preacher. I'm not going to put it in a counselor. I'm not going to put it in psychology. All these things could be God's means of bringing me relief and help, but my hope is ever and always in God."

2. A request for protection.

Confident in the Lord, the psalmist pleads, "Save me from all my transgressions; do not make me the scorn of fools." Today, he might say, "Lord, my confidence is in you, but I'm very shaky. I'm very angry. I'm very upset. I'm all torn up inside. This thing isn't going to get healed overnight. You're not going to touch me with a magic wand and then I'll be just fine. But, Lord, in the interim, while the healing is going on, don't let me do anything foolish so that I make matters infinitely worse."

3. An acceptance of God's sovereign will.

A dramatic thought occurs to the psalmist: "You, Lord, are the one who has done this." In today's voice he might say, "It just dawned on me. If you are the sovereign Lord, you were not out of control when these traumatic things happened. Therefore, in your will that is beyond my understanding, in your eternal purposes that are beyond my comprehension, you allowed these things. You knew they would discipline me and help me grow."

The sovereignty of God and the love of God are not mutually contradictory. We must hold them in tension, as the psalmist concluded. If an anger-inducing situation has come your way and you have handled it properly, is it true that you have deepened your relationship with God? Yes, it is. Is it true that you related to somebody in an extraordinary way? Yes, it is. Is it true that God was glorified in that extraordinary behavior? Yes, it is. Could it then be true to say that as the result of your responses and reactions in obedience and dependence to the Lord you have grown in a way you couldn't possibly have grown without these traumas? Yes, that is exactly the case. With God, all things are possible and good can come from bad.

From Rage to Rejoicing

With God's sovereignty in mind, we come to the concluding stanza of the psalmist's prayer:

> 12"Hear my prayer, O LORD,
>   listen to my cry for help;
>   be not deaf to my weeping.
>   For I dwell with you as an alien,
>   a stranger, as all my fathers were.
> 13Look away from me, that I may rejoice again
>   before I depart and am no more."

The writer pours out his hurt and acknowledges his dismay. Not least, he admits his feelings of estrangement from the Lord. So he asks the Lord to give him a break; to relieve the pain and ease off the pressure so that he might smile again. He knows his days are numbered and he'd like to end them with a smile rather than a scowl.

If we're not careful, we can form such a habit of anger, resentment, and bitterness that it becomes our pattern of life. What a tragedy, because we could be growing and maturing, developing and being renewed, particularly as we handle our hurt and anger properly. If your heart is burning with smoldering anger, don't repress or suppress it. Speak out to the Lord about it. If you feel alienated from God by your anger, cry out and ask him to draw you closer to himself. If the difficult experiences are past, ask yourself: Did I grow through them or did I sink into them?

The Lord does not rejoice in seeing you angry. He derives no pleasure from your living before him as an alien and a stranger. He much prefers a smile on your face to a scowl on your brow. May something positive and glorious result from these heart struggles as you put your hope and trust in God.

8

The Contrite Heart

Psalm 51

*Y*ears ago I had a young friend in England named Graham Stanford. To help make ends meet, Graham got a job working on a pipeline with some very rough men. He let his co-workers know that he was a Christian. They razzed him unmercifully, but Graham seemed totally impervious to it. One thing they all agreed on, however, was that a certain member of the crew, whom I will call Jake, was utterly and totally obnoxious. In most people's eyes he was beneath contempt.

All the guys would go to the pub frequently, and of course they spent their pay as soon as they got it. Then they would drink on credit for the next two weeks until they got their next paycheck. The accounts were kept on a chalkboard behind the bar so that everyone could see how much everyone else owed. Jake always had the biggest debt and he always carried debt over to the following week. He was getting further and further behind.

One day Graham went into the bar with the rest of the men, got a cloth, dampened it, walked around the bar, went up to the chalkboard, and wiped out Jake's name and his total indebtedness. Then Graham took his paycheck, handed it to the pub owner, and said, "Take it out of that." The other men stared; they couldn't believe their eyes.

They asked him, "Why in the world would you do that for him?"

Graham replied, "Because that's what God did for me. He forgave my sin. He wiped it out. It's no longer held against my name. It doesn't count."

That day was a turning point for all of those hardened and tough men. Forgiveness is a powerful thing. Unfortunately some of us never experience it. We prefer to hold on to the deep, dark secrets of our heart rather than coming clean and allowing God to change us. How do we receive forgiveness and how do we offer it? As we continue this study of the secrets of the heart, Psalm 51 speaks dramatically about the prerequisite for forgiveness: a broken and contrite heart.

A Broken and Contrite Heart

King David was a man who knew about forgiveness. He had an enormous debt of sin after his affair with Bathsheba and the murder of her husband. After he was confronted with his sin, David wrote Psalm 51 in response. In it he uses the word *contrite*. This word is not in common usage today as much as it ought to be. I checked on the dictionary definition and to be contrite is "to be deeply affected with grief and sorrow for having done wrong." In this particular psalm, David is very affected and concerned, and he wants to talk to the Lord about what is going on in his life.

> [1]Have mercy on me, O God,
>   according to your unfailing love;
>   according to your great compassion
>   blot out my transgressions.

²Wash away all my iniquity
    and cleanse me from my sin.

³For I know my transgressions,
    and my sin is always before me.
⁴Against you, you only, have I sinned
    and done what is evil in your sight,
  so that you are proved right when you speak
    and justified when you judge.

    .   .   .   .

¹⁶You do not delight in sacrifice, or I would bring it;
    you do not take pleasure in burnt offerings.
¹⁷The sacrifices of God are a broken spirit;
    a broken and contrite heart,
    O God, you will not despise.

In some Bibles there is a brief introduction to the circumstances under which this psalm was written. We're told it was "for the director of music," and was given to musicians to put to music. It was "a psalm of David," assuming that it was written by David or for David. The situation was when the prophet Nathan came to him after David had committed adultery with Bathsheba. This act was a deep, dark secret in the heart of King David. He had done the most appalling series of things and he had engaged in a massive cover-up.

During all this, however, he had apparently continued all religious observances. On the outside, he was doing everything absolutely right—he was a good religious person. But on the inside it was an entirely different story.

Excruciating Honesty

God eventually sent the prophet Nathan to let David know that God looked on the inside of David's heart, and the dark secret was exposed. It was a traumatic experience for David, recounted in 2 Samuel 12. Today's media would have had a heyday. This was a story of sex and violence, lust and adultery, murder and cover up, national scandal and deception in high places. The situation, however, had to be dealt with.

The reason that this psalm, of course, is tremendously beneficial to us is that to a greater or lesser extent we all have the capability of living on the outside the righteous religious life while maintaining within our deep, dark secrets. Our "double lives" need to be dealt with.

In a parallel psalm, Psalm 32, King David explained what he went through while he insisted on the cover-up. "When I kept silent, my bones wasted away through my groaning all day long. For day and night your hand was heavy upon me; my strength was sapped as in the heat of summer" (Ps. 32:3-4).

What a graphic description. In other words, when he was in the cover-up frame of mind, his guilt sapped everything out of him. Most of us know what it is like to be utterly worn out in the oppressive heat of summer. In a similar way, do you know what it is to be spiritually sapped of energy? Perhaps the reason for our spiritual lack of energy and enthusiasm is directly related to a deep, dark secret that we're covering up and not dealing with, all the while going through righteous religious motions.

In order to deal with his secret sin, David's next step was crucial, "Then I acknowledged my sin to you and did not cover up my iniquity. I said, 'I will confess my transgressions to the LORD'" (Ps. 32:5).

There is a great need for all of us in one form or another to come before the Lord with excruciating honesty if we are to know his renewal, regeneration, restoration, and refreshment in our lives. But so often we tend to hold onto, even cherish the secret things. We cling to them even though we know that they are abhorrent in the eyes of God, contrary to his best plans for us, and that they are robbing us of his blessing. With this in mind, let's touch on the salient points of Psalm 51.

The Truth about Sin

David opens with a cry for forgiveness, "Have mercy on me, O God, according to your unfailing love; according to your great compassion blot out my transgressions. Wash away all my iniquity and cleanse me from my sin" (vss. 1-2). Notice first of all an acknowledgment of sin. David does not say, "Hey, I know I'm no angel, but I have never pretended to be perfect. I have made my mistakes; there have been certain errors of judgment." That is modern parlance and is the best that many of us can do in dealing with the deep, dark secrets of the heart. We're not talking about making mistakes; we're talking transgression, iniquity, and sin.

God has outlined for us in numerous places things that we should not do. Human beings, however, have an innate desire to do these things. *Transgression* is willfully defying God and doing what he categorically has told us not to do. Every time we have done that which God says thou shalt not do, we have transgressed.

The term *iniquity* refers to perverting or polluting that which is inherently or innately good. Think of all the beautiful things that God has given us. What have we done to love? We've confused it with lust. What have we done with the institution of the family, intended to be the loving environment in which we bring people to maturity? Instead of being a nest of nurture, all too often the family has become the crucible of confusion and chaos. What have we done to marriage? At least half the marriages embarked upon finish up in divorce. What have we done to worship? What have we done to communion? What have we done with prayer? What have we done with the environment? By our iniquity and sin we have been guilty of perverting and polluting that which is good.

What is sin? *Sin* means "to miss the mark." In Judges 20:16 we read about some very skilled Israelite soldiers who "were left-handed, each of whom could sling a stone at a hair and not miss." The Hebrew word used here for "miss" is the same word used in other places for "sin." Sin is missing the target. God has also given us things he's told us to do, and we're always missing the mark. God says, "Love me all your heart and love your neighbor as yourself." We shrug our shoulders and say, "God, that's unrealistic. You are asking us for too much. We can't do it." We miss the mark, and God calls it sin.

We blatantly expect to get away with what God has straightforwardly forbidden us to do. We think that we have the inalienable right to take that which is inherently good from the hand of a gracious God and ruin it and there will be no consequences. God says we're wrong. Men and women need to come to terms with the fact that in their own hearts they have a remarkable capacity for transgression, iniquity, and sin. We must acknowledge it.

Notice, however, that in this cry for forgiveness there is also an admittance of unworthiness. If we go on a guilt trip or feel a sense of shame about what we've done, sometimes we'll get worried about it and pray. The approach, however, often takes this tack: "God, I'm not perfect. I've made mistakes. I'm paying for my errors. But I've done a lot of good things, too, so I hope that you'll be decent about this. I hope that you'll be fair enough to count all the good stuff I've done and bounce it up against the bad stuff, and that I'll make it by the skin of my teeth." That is exactly how *not* to go about it.

Incredible Grace

What a parody the above approach is when we begin to understand that our only hope is the incredible grace, mercy, and compassion of God. Look how the psalmist does it. He says, in effect, "God, I cannot come to you on the basis of my achievements because, when I look at them, they're shot through with iniquity and transgression and sin. I come to you not on the basis of my attainment.

I come to you on the basis of your unmerited favor, your incredible compassion, your overwhelming mercy, and your superlative grace. I understand that if there is any hope of my being spiritually renewed, restored, refreshed, and regenerated, it is going to be dependent on who you are and not on what I am."

Notice that in verses 1-2 the psalmist talks about forgiveness in three ways: "blot out my transgressions," "wash away all my iniquity," and "cleanse me from my sin." All three are pictures of complete and total forgiveness. When we think in terms of forgiveness, we do not come to God trying to make a case for how good we are. Rather, we come and ask for mercy and grace. We say, "God, because you are the kind of God you are and despite the kind of person I am, would you wipe it out?" The great good news is this: God doesn't merely dampen a cloth with water to wipe off our debt from the chalkboard; he dampens the cloth with the blood of his Son, and through the Cross he makes forgiveness possible.

"Blot out my transgressions," David prayed. The term for "blot out" is close to the meaning of "wipe away." This reminds us that Graham Stanford's actions of literally wiping away his friend's debt off the chalkboard was a powerful symbol of God's actions toward us.

"Wash away my iniquity," he implored. The word translated "wash away" is the old-fashioned word for *laundry*. The method for doing the laundry in ancient societies—and in some places to this day—was to take the dirty clothes down to the river and pummel them in the water on the smooth rocks. He is asking God to deal with this deep-down stain and pummel it out. When we think in terms of God's mercy and grace, we think of the pummeling that Christ took on the cross in order that the deep stain of our sin might be washed out.

"Cleanse me from my sin," David asks. There were certain people in the Old Testament who were barred from worship because of activities in which they had been en-

gaged that rendered them "unclean." They were disqualified from the place of worship, for instance, if they'd touched a dead body or if they had contracted leprosy. But after a certain period of time, they could go through a ritualistic cleansing process and the disqualification was taken away. That's the word for *cleanse* that the psalmist uses here. We can imagine him saying, "There are certain things that I have done in my heart that I have been covering up, and they disqualified me from an intimate relationship with you. O God, please take away the things that disqualified me. Deal with these issues, and let me be renewed, refreshed, restored, and regenerated." All of us can identify with what the psalmist is saying here. Each of us may cry for forgiveness.

Whatever Happened to Sin?

Look again at David's straightforward confession, "For I know my transgressions, and my sin is always before me" (vs. 3). These words reveal that David had a sense of continual awareness of his sin. In the old days preachers called this "conviction of sin," a deep-down, inner sense of uneasiness. To be convicted of sin is to have a sensitive conscience, pricked by the Holy Spirit, resulting in a willingness to call sin sin.

The eminent psychiatrist Karl Menninger wrote a book simply entitled *Whatever Became of Sin?* What has happened to sin? Despite all the great benefits of psychology, sociology, and anthropology which have helped us to understand human behavior, the downside of this knowledge is that we tend to psychologize our behavior. Bad behavior and unfortunate aberrations are the result of our upbringing in dysfunctional families. That may be true, but in the end, when our behavior contravenes what God has said, it needs to be called sin. My sin is not just the result of my dysfunctional upbringing; it is downright disobedience, downright lack of faith, downright unbelief. Unless I come to that consciousness, I am living a cover-up.

We all need reality checks in this regard. That is what happens to the psalmist here. He knows his transgressions; his sin is always before him. If we haven't come to terms with that fact, then we haven't begun to understand the fundamental truth of spiritual life. Admitting our sin is the beginning of living in reality.

Sinning against Whom?

David goes on to explain that, "Against you [God], you only, have I sinned and done what is evil in your sight" (vs. 4). Now that's a very strange thing to say. Why would he say that? He certainly had sinned against Bathsheba and against her husband, Uriah. He had sinned in lying to the prophet and in his deception to the people. David had sinned against more people than you could shake a stick at.

If we really want to go places in our walk with God and really deal with our sin, it has to be more than just feeling badly for ourselves or for hurting others. We must also feel contrite because we have sinned against God. Our transgressions are wrong for the very simple reason that it is God who defines evil, and not us. In our better moments we realize our actions have hurt ourselves and have abused others. But what really counts is that we have ultimately sinned against God.

David is coming to terms with guilt—real guilt, not a guilt trip imposed upon him by other people. Verse 4 continues, "Against you, you only, have I sinned and done what is evil in your sight, so that you are proved right when you speak and justified when you judge." Many people assume that because God is a God of love and a God of grace, it will all come out in the wash. If you suggest that there may be such a thing as judgment, they become deeply offended, even angry. They might say that you are hopelessly out of date to believe in a God who judges: "If God is a God of love, how could he ever do that?"

The response to this, of course, is, "If God is a God of justice, righteousness, and holiness, how could he fail to judge?" The psalmist starts off talking about the mercy and great compassion of God and then says, "But, God, you are proved right when you speak, and you are totally justified when you judge. Because I'm really guilty and I totally agree with your judgment of me. You're right and I'm wrong." That is the response of a contrite heart.

Hope for Renewal

"Surely you desire truth in the inner parts," David prays in verse 6. The word *truth* here means literally "loyalty." God made people so that they would be loyal to him; that they would love, honor, and serve him and live in relationship to him and experience his blessing. Unfortunately the wheel came off the cart. The Fall happened. Sin entered into the world. We are all infected and instead of an inner loyalty to God, we have an inner proclivity to sin and disloyalty. Is there any hope? Here is a call for renewal:

> 7Cleanse me with hyssop, and I will be clean;
>> wash me, and I will be whiter than snow.
> 8Let me hear joy and gladness;
>> let the bones you have crushed rejoice.
> 9Hide your face from my sins
>> and blot out all my iniquity.
> 10Create in me a pure heart, O God,
>> and renew a steadfast spirit within me.
> 11Do not cast me from your presence
>> or take your Holy Spirit from me.
> 12Restore to me the joy of your salvation
>> and grant me a willing spirit, to sustain me.

We can ask God to renew us. We can pray that by his mercy, grace, and loving kindness he would give us what we don't deserve and forgive and restore us. God isn't just interested in getting the load of guilt off us. He wants to make us new so that we might live as we were intended to live all along. He delights in the plea of verse 10: "Create in me a pure heart, O God, and renew a steadfast spirit within me."

We talk about artistic people being "creative," but strictly speaking, no human being is creative. Only God creates. Creative human beings take that which God has created and, in an innovative way, make it into something else. Here, the contrite heart of Psalm 51 is appealing to the Creator. He says in effect, "Restore me to a right relationship with you so that I can begin to be what I'm supposed to be—which will take a miracle of re-creation in my life. As you created the heavens and the earth, you'd better do a number on me." Is God working in your life in this way? Have things happened in you that are explicable only in terms of God's power moving and working?

Steadfast and New

Someone has said that when divine action takes place, it brings forth something new and astonishing. That's what David is asking for—a new and astonishing steadfast spirit, which means an inner disposition of loyalty to and consistency before God.

David wants to turn his back on all the other stuff. Put right what's wrong. Get things in order. Rectify the things that he had no business doing. Do the things he should have done, because God has renewed in him an entirely different attitude that is attributable only to a creative work of God himself. He desires a steadfast spirit within him. Verse 11 gives us a clue to what this spirit is: "Do not cast me from your presence or take your Holy Spirit from me."

This steadfast spirit within us is directly related to the work of the Holy Spirit within us. The death of Christ procured forgiveness for us. The sending of the Holy Spirit into our hearts procured our renewal and revival. The word *spirit* in the Old Testament comes from the Hebrew word *ruach,* meaning "breath." It has the idea of a moving force, a life-giving force, a breath being exhaled.

A spirit brings up images of a life-giving, energizing force. When we consider that this spirit is holy, we're reminded that it comes from an awe-inspiring God. When we think of the Holy Spirit coming into our lives and renewing a right spirit within us, what we're thinking of is a life-giving dynamic coming from God himself that will produce within us a great sense of awe. We want then to honor and to please the Lord.

Read on in verse 12: "Restore to me the joy of your salvation." David wants the sheer enthusiasm, the sheer exuberance of knowing God. I worry about people who show incredible enthusiasm about material things, such as making money or wearing the latest styles, but who have no interest at all in the things of God.

David also asks, in verse 12, "grant me a willing spirit to sustain me." This inner disposition born of the Holy Spirit results in a generous volunteer spirit. Some churches try all kinds of ways of recruiting people to do what they don't want to do. There's a better way: bring people to an understanding of grace, to a contrite and broken heart, to renewal in the Holy Spirit. What happens? They become exuberant about God and develop a generous spirit; they volunteer out of sheer gratitude to serve the living and true God.

Verse 13 follows naturally: "Then I will teach transgressors your ways, and sinners will turn back to you." Churches have all kinds of evangelism programs trying to get people to knock on doors they don't want to knock on, give out literature they don't want to give out, accost people in shopping malls that they don't want to accost. There's a better way. With a contrite heart, a renewed spirit, a sense of forgiveness and of being overwhelmed by God's grace, people will be motivated. Out of the sheer thrill of what it means to be forgiven, they will go and say,

"Let me tell you how you can be forgiven and what it's like to be blessed out of your socks." A new generous, volunteer spirit will come when God's Spirit works in our hearts.

From Brokenness to Praise

David was so busy keeping up external appearances that he wouldn't admit the dark secrets in his heart. Finally, the prophet Nathan let David know that God knew all about it. David came to deep conviction of his sin, and he turned from it. He prayed, "O God, in your great grace and mercy restore, renew, revive me. And do a work of grace in my life that will make me the kind of person who exalts and praises you." That's what a contrite heart looks like. And the result? God will be praised.

> 15O Lord, open my lips,
>   and my mouth will declare your praise.
> 16You do not delight in sacrifice, or I would bring it;
>   you do not take pleasure in burnt offerings.
> 17The sacrifices of God are a broken spirit;
>   a broken and contrite heart,
>   O God, you will not despise.

These last two verses reveal the fact that the psalmist has experienced such a work of grace in his own heart that his desire is that others might experience it too. The process of repentance and forgiveness frees us and feeds us spiritually. The more excited you are about the Lord, the more excited you are that others should be excited about him.

There's much we can learn about the heart. There's no more important lesson, however, than the fact that God is looking for a repentant, broken, and contrite heart. Then, in his great mercy, he can do his work of renewal.

And what a work of renewal it is! Guilt is banished,

shame is taken away, fellowship is restored, and vision is revived. A new vigor is exhibited, a new concern demonstrated. Openness of heart takes the place of cover-up and deceit. Burdens are lifted and the spirit takes wing. Why would anyone prefer estrangement through unconfessed sin to the joy of living in harmony with God?

9
The Steadfast Heart
Psalm 57

a friend of mine once said that he had an 18-inch gap in his spiritual experience. I was intrigued to hear someone be so precise about the measurement. He explained that at one stage of his life there had been a gap between what he *knew* in his head and what he *felt* 18 inches lower in his heart. And this "missed connection" caused problems with his actions and attitudes.

Many of us could probably testify to a spiritual gap in our experience at times. It is perfectly possible for us to have a head knowledge of matters of faith but not really feel deeply about them in our hearts. While we recognize the phenomenon and fully understand how this happens, it's important to be clear in our understanding of what the Bible really means by the *heart*.

Heart, Mind, and Will

We tend to think of the heart as the center of our emotions and feelings. When the Bible talks about the heart, however, it has a much broader view. It talks about the heart as the center of the will and the mind as well as the emotions. In other words, the heart discerns with the mind, it desires with the emotions, and it decides with the will.

Because we are fallen human beings and our hearts are less than perfect, we find ourselves confusing truth and error. Tainted by pride, we may desire what is inappropriate. With our minds we may appreciate the truthfulness of what God has said, but with our emotions we may desire the opposite. We may want desperately to do something even though we know that God has advised against it. Even our wills are affected by sin, so at times we choose not to do what, deep down, we know we ought to do. We have a problem with the heart.

In Psalm 57, however, we read something very helpful. The psalmist tells us that he has a "steadfast heart." He has a heart that is settled, fixed, determined, established. He has a heart that understands what is right and also desires to do it. He has a heart that decides that the right thing is what he will do. Furthermore, having made these decisions based on what he discerns with his mind and desires with his will, he sticks with it.

Steadfast, Not Wobbly

We're all painfully aware of the fact that our culture lacks steadfastness. People sign contracts and when events do not turn out the way they want them to, they want to renegotiate. People make commitments but if it is not convenient to fulfill the commitment, they walk away. People promise to help with something but if it's a nice day, they don't bother showing up. People stand at the front of a church and make marriage vows, "Until death us do part," but discover that long before death parts them their spouse has upset or disappointed them. They don't want to be married any more, so they walk away from it.

Often, changing circumstances make it difficult for us to discern clearly, desire properly, and decide rightly. At other times, even if we have understood what is right, desired what is right, and made wise decisions, the circumstances are such that we simply renege on commitments. So how do we grow in steadfastness? We need to help and encourage each other in this area.

British Prime Minister Margaret Thatcher was once invited to the White House to be honored for her friendship and support of Presidents Reagan and Bush. President Bush related a story about Thatcher during the Persian Gulf War. United States officials had been ambivalent and were beginning to think, "It's all right going in, but how are we going to get out?" They were getting estimates from the Pentagon and other places on how many casualties to expect. They were wondering how they were going to explain going into somewhere called Kuwait, which most people had to look in an atlas to find.

Margaret Thatcher called President Bush one day and said, as only she could, "George, this is no time to get wobbly." I think sometimes we need the Maggie Thatchers of this world to tell us to stop being wobbly. We need people with steadfast hearts.

Psalm 57 gives us a wonderful example of a person who in an utterly calamitous set of circumstances was still able to say that his heart was fixed and steadfast. The psalmist didn't say, "God, get me out of this calamity and then I will have a steadfast heart." Rather, he affirmed, "I will take refuge in you right now." Listen to what he wrote:

> [1]Have mercy on me, O God, have mercy on me,
>   for in you my soul takes refuge.
> I will take refuge in the shadow of your wings
>   until the disaster has passed.
>
> [2]I cry out to God Most High,
>   to God, who fulfills his purpose for me.

3He sends from heaven and saves me,
   rebuking those who hotly pursue me;
   God sends his love and his faithfulness.

4I am in the midst of lions;
   I lie among ravenous beasts—
men whose teeth are spears and arrows,
   whose tongues are sharp swords.

5Be exalted, O God, above the heavens;
   let your glory be over all the earth.

6They spread a net for my feet—
   I was bowed down in distress.
They dug a pit in my path—
   but they have fallen into it themselves.

7My heart is steadfast, O God,
   my heart is steadfast;
   I will sing and make music.
8Awake, my soul!
   Awake, harp and lyre!
   I will awaken the dawn.

9I will praise you, O Lord, among the nations;
   I will sing of you among the peoples.
10For great is your love, reaching to the heavens;
   your faithfulness reaches to the skies.

11Be exalted, O God, above the heavens;
   let your glory be over all the earth.

What were the awful circumstances—the "ravenous beasts" and the deep "pit"—the psalmist was experiencing here? Some Bibles report that this was written when David "had fled from Saul into the cave." But the story of this psalm starts long before that.

David's Dangerous Predicament

The nation of Israel had a strong enemy, the Philistines, who had a champion by the name of Goliath. This giant suggested that each nation pick a champion, let them fight, and the outcome would decide which nation wins. The Israelites looked at Goliath and decided that was no way to go. Their king, Saul, the first king they'd ever had, was a superb physical specimen. He was the likely man to respond to Goliath's challenge, but he took one look at Goliath, said that he was too big to hit with anything, and cowered in his tent.

One day a young boy, David, visited his older brothers in the army. He heard Goliath present his challenge, and he looked around expecting somebody to respond. But nobody did. Young David was taken aback. When he looked at Goliath, he saw a giant who was too big to miss. He obviously had a different point of view than Saul's.

David volunteered to fight Goliath, and King Saul let him. When David arrived, Goliath said, "Who do you think you are? Do you think I'm a dog that you send somebody like you to fight me?" David replied, "No, I don't think you're a dog. I think you're a very big giant, and I've come to get you." He took his sling and fired a stone straight at Goliath. The stone went like a bullet, hit the giant in the forehead, and knocked him unconscious. David jumped up, grabbed the giant's sword, killed him, and chopped off his head.

Now King Saul was embarrassed to death about David's victory, as you can understand. He didn't have the moral fortitude, however, to admit that he'd been wrong and that David was right. He just began to get envious, particularly when David returned home and all the young women in town thought he was the greatest thing that had ever happened. They had a special procession for him. They wrote songs for him. They danced with him. King Saul was furious because they sang, "Saul has killed his thousands, but

David his tens of thousands." Now, their arithmetic wasn't so good, but you get their drift—and Saul certainly did. He became insanely jealous of David.

People warned David to get out of town and that the king was after his hide. So David took off into the wilderness, hunted and hounded from pillar to post. To make matters worse, four hundred people—who were in all kinds of debt, discouragement, and discontent—sought out David as their leader. So not only did David have King Saul and three thousand soldiers chasing him, he had nowhere to live and four hundred needy people following him around.

You see David's problem? Somebody was insanely jealous of him. He was in fear of his life. He had nowhere to go; no one to help him. What was he to do?

I can imagine one possibility. David could have said to these people, "I've had it up to here with you people who expect me to be solving your problems when I've got more problems than I can shake a stick at myself. I have had it with King Saul—he's crazy and dangerous. I'm through with this country. I'm through with you people. And, God, though we made a covenant, I'm through with you. I'm out of here."

Instead, what did David do? He wrote a psalm and proclaimed, "My heart is steadfast, O my God. My heart is steadfast." He was saying that in the midst of this calamitous situation, he was absolutely convinced of some things. There were certain things that he had discerned, desired, and decided, and his heart and will were of the caliber that he was going to stick with God through hell or high water.

Discerning God As Our Refuge

There's a fistful of things in Psalm 57 that David discerns about God. One is that David knows who his true refuge is in times of trouble: "Have mercy on me, O God, . . .

for in you my soul takes refuge" (vs. 1). He can't trust the king and he can't get any help from the people hanging around his neck, but he is certain he can take refuge in the Lord. Then he uses a very dramatic expression: "I will take refuge in the shadow of your wings."

In the Old Testament God had allowed himself to be portrayed as an eagle who, under his mighty wings, sheltered his young. Psalm 91 uses the metaphor of God having feathers and protecting his people under his wings. In the New Testament, the Lord Jesus referred to himself as a sort of mother hen who wanted to gather the people of Jerusalem "under his wings." The image is very obvious: those who really trusted the Lord saw him as the One who was a loving, stable refuge when everything around them was unstable and unreliable.

David, of course, knew about the tabernacle—the portable temple of worship that the Israelites had carried with them in their wilderness journeys. (Later King David would plan to build a more permanent temple, which his son Solomon actually constructed.) But in the tabernacle there was a section called the Holy of Holies, where only the high priest was allowed to enter and meet with the presence of God. This place of meeting held the Ark of the Covenant, which had carved over it two cherubim whose wings were folded over in protection. Perhaps David had this image in mind when he wrote, "I will take refuge in the shadow of your wings." He knew there was only one place where a sinful person could be reconciled to a holy God. It was in that holy place of God's choosing that he found shelter.

We read in verse 2, "I cry out to God Most High, to God, who fulfills his purpose for me." Prayers are only as effective as the One to whom they're directed. To whom does he direct his prayers? The Hebrew name here is *El Elyon,* "God, Most High." David is saying in effect that he knew God, the King of kings, the Lord of lords, and that he could find refuge in him. Why? Because God was his protector and had a purpose for his life.

God's purposes will be worked out even in the cave, even in the dark times, even at the time of disaster, even in calamitous situations. Have you discovered and discerned this truth? Is your heart fixed on these things? Is the Lord your shelter, the one immovable factor of your life? Is that something that you hold on to whatever the circumstances might be?

If you're wondering how you can do that, read on: "He sends from heaven and saves me, rebuking those who hotly pursue me. God sends his love and his faithfulness" (vs. 3). Do you know deep down in your heart that God loves you and is faithfully committed to you whatever the circumstances might be? Today, you can be certain of this commitment because of the Cross of Christ, for there is no better picture of God's love and faithfulness to you. God so loved you that he gave his only begotten Son to die for you. Learn from David's life.

Desiring God's Glory

What did David's heart desire? In the middle of this psalm he breaks off twice and declares, "Be exalted, O God, above the heavens; let your glory be over all the earth" (vss. 5, 11). At the moment of disaster his concern was not "Get me out of this disaster" or "Deliver me from this calamity!" His concern was that God be honored. He was saying, "God, in the midst of this calamitous situation, in some incredible way, be glorified. Do something in my life that is going to be attributable only to divine intervention, so that men and women, even cynics, will say that only God could have fixed things."

Most of us today don't say this in quite same way. But we do say, "Our Father, who art in heaven, hallowed be thy name. Thy kingdom come, thy will be done on earth as it is in heaven." When we pray this way, we are saying, "Lord, in this calamitous mess, in this incredible situation that I'm in right now, I know who you are. My heart is fixed on what I discern and on what I desire. I want your name to be honored. Because of that ultimate desire of my heart, I have decided that I will stick with the decisions that I have made."

Deciding to Trust

Spiritual experience is based on divine initiative. If God had not chosen to create humanity and then to provide redemption, there would be neither a human story nor a salvation saga. God has acted but we are called to respond; we react. And that requires an act of the will. The psalmist understood and referred to this in his writings.

Recurring in this psalm are two little words: *I will.*

- ❏ "I will take refuge." (vs. 1)

- ❏ "I will sing and make music." (vs. 7)

- ❏ "I will awaken the dawn." (vs. 8)

- ❏ "I will praise you, O Lord, among the nations." (vs. 9)

- ❏ "I will sing of you among the peoples." (vs. 9)

"I will do these things," David affirms. This is what he had decided; it was settled; it was fixed; it was established. His heart was steadfast. Our world needs people like that. Consider a written testimony of a young anonymous pastor in Zimbabwe, found in his office after he had been martyred in 1994.

I'm part of the fellowship of the unashamed. I have the Holy Spirit's power. The die has been cast. I have stepped over the line. The decision has been made. I'm a disciple of His. I won't look back, let up, slow down, back away, or be still. My past is redeemed. My present makes sense. My future is secure. I'm finished and done with low living, sight walking, smooth knees, colorless dreams, tame visions, worldly talking, cheap giving, and dwarfed goals.

I no longer need preeminence, prosperity, position, promotions, plaudits, or popularity. I don't have to be right. I don't have to be first. I don't have to be tops. I don't have to be recognized. I don't have to be praised. I don't have to be regarded. I don't have to be rewarded. I now live by faith. I lean on His presence. I walk by patience. I'm uplifted by prayer, and I labor with power.

My face is set. My gait is fast. My goal is heaven. My road is narrow. My way is rough. My companions are few. My guide is reliable. My mission is clear. I cannot be bought, compromised, detoured, lured away, turned back, deluded, or delayed.

I will not flinch in the face of sacrifice, hesitate in the presence of the enemy, pander at the pool of popularity, or meander in the maze of mediocrity. I won't give up, shut up, let up until I've stayed up, stored up, prayed up, paid up, and preached up.

I am a disciple of Jesus. I must go till He comes, give till I drop, preach till all know, and work till He stops me. And when He comes for His own, He'll have no problem recognizing me. My banner will be clear.

Those words could only come from a committed, steadfast heart. Do you have a steadfast heart? One that is firmly fixed in place, not subject to change, firm in belief, forever faithful? What keeps you from it? Life can be so hard and we often just look for the easy way out. We get upset when things don't go the way we want them to go, and we believe that we deserve something better.

We overlook the fact that we are sinful people living in

a fallen and uncertain world. God is the one certainty we can depend on. In love he beckons us to turn to him in the midst of distress, and to find in him a life of trust and praise. May he do a work in our sinful, fickle hearts that will make us more steadfast men and women of faith.

10
The Wise Heart
Psalm 90

There are two inescapable realities that human beings face: death and evil. Our discomfort with these realities is seen in the proliferation of new crime bills and heftier police forces, as well as the rise in concern about health care reform and the staggering growth of the health and exercise industry. We all want to live longer and be insulated and safe from evil while we're doing it. But the Bible suggests a different way of facing reality: living with a heart of wisdom.

True Wisdom

In Old Testament days, the Hebrew word used for "wisdom" was *hokmah* and originally meant a "skill of any kind." For example, a wise sailor would be one who could skillfully navigate treacherous waters. A wise judge was one who had the skill of dealing with a very complex issue. A wise artisan was one who was skilled at creating beautiful artifacts. As time went on, wisdom came to mean more specifically the spiritual skill to discern God's purposes, the desire to do them, and the ability to fulfill them. Wisdom, therefore, is actually the practical knowledge and ability to do what God wants us to do.

In Psalm 90:12 we find this definition of wisdom used clearly: "Teach us to number our days aright, that we may gain a heart of wisdom." The psalmist might just as easily have prayed, "Teach us to number our days aright, that we may gain a heart that has insights into what God wants us to do, and that has the desire and the ability to do it."

Why is the psalmist so concerned about numbering his days rightly? Why is he so concerned about finding out if he's living as he ought to live? The beginning of Psalm 90 gives us some answers.

The Basics of Our Beliefs

The writer begins this psalm by reaffirming some basic beliefs:

> ¹Lord, you have been our dwelling place
>   throughout all generations.
> ²Before the mountains were born
>   or you brought forth the earth and the world,
>   from everlasting to everlasting you are God.

Everyone has what I call "basic beliefs." We will believe many different things on different levels, but undergirding all of our beliefs will be one or two fundamental, basic beliefs. Let me identify some of these for you.

One basic belief for many people is *God is.* The basic belief for many other people is *God isn't.* Whichever of these you believe, you will then build a whole system of beliefs that will lead to certain behaviors. This explains one of the major problems confronting our culture: we have grave difficulty having any kind of dialogue with people who differ from us because there is no commonality of basic beliefs.

Note that this psalm is a prayer to the "Lord." The Hebrew word used here for "Lord" is *Adonai* (different from *Jehovah,* used in other places for "LORD"). *Adonai* means "controller, sustainer, and Creator of the universe." This definition sheds some light on the psalmist's basic belief in who God is. Some people believe that the universe is infinite—without beginning, without end. Others say that the universe clearly is winding down, that it therefore had a beginning, and that something or someone began it. Such people—I among them—believe there is a Creator and a controller of the universe.

Incidentally, the Bible doesn't debate this topic or discuss it. It simply starts out with the assumption, "In the beginning God." (Gen. 1:1). No discussion. No argument. Just this fundamental, basic belief. This is where the psalmist starts out as well—with the existence of a Lord and Master, a controller and sustainer of the universe.

We Can Experience God

But notice that the psalmist goes further. He talks about the personal experience that he and his people have had with this grand controller of the universe. "Lord," he says, "you have been *our* dwelling place throughout all generations" (italics added).

Because Psalm 90 was written by Moses, it is one of the oldest psalms available to us. Moses lived 120 years, which divided rather neatly into three periods. He spent the first forty years in Egypt, where the Israelites had been enslaved for four hundred years. Born a Hebrew, he was under a death threat as a male baby, and his mother maneuvered events so that he was actually brought up in Pharaoh's court. He wasn't born with a silver spoon in his mouth, but he got one very quickly.

Then, unfortunately, he killed a man and had to flee for his life. He spent forty years in exile. Finally, he was recalled to a place of prominence, led the children of Israel through a conflict with Pharaoh out of Egypt, and spent the next forty years with the Israelites in the wilderness.

At 120 years of age he was able to climb up Mount Nebo, from which he saw the most beautiful vista—the Promised Land. Having spent forty years in a barren wilderness, he saw the fertile valley of the Jordan River, the Dead Sea, and the beautiful oasis of Jericho down below him. He knew that the children of Israel would be going into that land of milk and honey.

So when the psalmist speaks about "all generations," perhaps he was thinking of a generation that lived in the lap of luxury; a generation that lived in exile; a generation that lived victimized as slaves. He could see a generation that was going to experience divine blessing. In short, he had had a very wide set of experiences. He does not dwell, however, on his various experiences, but concentrates on the constant factor in the changing experiences—that in all of them the Lord was his dwelling place.

Isn't this a comfort for us? It doesn't really matter whether you were born with a silver spoon in your mouth, whether you were victimized, whether you are living in exile, or whether you are living in a place of great spiritual blessing. What really matters is that in all these situations you have a relationship with the Controller and the Sustainer of the universe so that you can say at all times, "I find my security, I find my shelter, I find my resources in the Lord."

God Is Eternal

Thinking of who the Lord is, the psalmist then states, "Before the mountains were born or you brought forth the earth and the world"—clear statements concerning God's creative activity—"from everlasting to everlasting you are

God." Don't try to think on this too hard because you've got a finite mind that has problems with infinite concepts. But what the psalmist is saying is this: before the mountains were made, before the earth was created, there was a bygone eternity. He is not talking about an infinite universe but about an infinite God who has continually existed.

Moses declares, "From everlasting to everlasting you *are* God." Not "from everlasting you *were* to everlasting you will be." He is talking about the God of creation, the God of the ages, the God who is utterly eternal without beginning, without end, immutable, unchanging, totally reliable, the one constant factor in human experience.

Without apology, these are the basic beliefs of which the Bible speaks. I ask you carefully to consider whether they are yours. Take time to reaffirm your basic beliefs, to reflect upon them. One of the things in dramatic short supply in our culture is the opportunity and the desire for quiet reflection, the opportunity to lay aside legitimate concerns and activities and simply take the time quietly and thoughtfully to ponder and reflect upon matters of incredible significance. Our lives are swamped with trivialities.

Do you take the time to reflect on the basic issues of your faith? Do you take time to reaffirm your basic beliefs? The psalmist does. In fact, it is when he reaffirms his basic beliefs—which leads him inevitably to reflection on basic issues—that he says, "O Lord, teach me to number my days." In other words, "You'd better teach me to get my act together. And to do that, I need a heart of wisdom." Have you got your act together? Have you got your basic beliefs squared away? Are you carefully thinking through the basic issues that come from those basic beliefs?

Life Is Short and Death Is Certain

The first issue that comes immediately to Moses' mind is the brevity of life. This is how he puts it in verses 3-6:

3You turn men back to dust,
    saying, "Return to dust, O sons of men."
4For a thousand years in your sight
    are like a day that has just gone by,
    or like a watch in the night.
5You sweep men away in the sleep of death;
    they are like the new grass of the morning—
6though in the morning it springs up new,
    by evening it is dry and withered.

The psalmist is talking about a basic issue that a lot of people want to avoid and evade: life is extremely brief in the light of eternity. If we are thinking of a God who is from eternity to eternity, then what we experience of life is an infinitesimal fragment, and we must see it in its proper perspective.

Many hundreds of years ago, Christian missionaries first arrived in the north of England, a wild piece of territory inhabited by wild people—the area, incidentally, from which I come, which may help explain some things. The missionaries were invited to sit down and discuss their new message with King Edwin of Northumbria at a council that he called in a town rejoicing in the name of Godmundingham. They met in a large castle, and the Christian missionaries presented their story. The king had invited the wise people of the neighborhood to come in and decide whether they wanted to listen to this strange new message. One of the heathens, a man called Thane, got up and said:

> Your majesty, did you perceive that whilst we were sitting by your roaring fire enjoying the feasting in your castle that a little bird flew in from the violent storm outside and for one brief moment flew through the room of our castle until it flew out the other side back into the bitter cold and the raging storm outside?
> Our life is like that. For one brief, bright moment

we're alive. We know nothing of the storm. We know nothing of what lies ahead. Therefore, if this man has a message that will tell us what went before and what comes after, we need to hear him!

I want to suggest that the proper perspective is to think of our lives as birds flying out of the storm, across a warm room, and flying out the other side into the unknown—unless we have developed a heart of wisdom. Notice that when we begin to think of the brevity of life, we automatically think of another very unpopular subject, death. In poetic language, the psalmist phrases it: "You turn people back to dust, saying, 'Return to dust!' . . . You sweep people away like dreams that disappear" (Ps. 90:3, 5, *New Living Translation*).

Those of you who have attended a committal service of a funeral may have been somewhat puzzled when the minister said, "Dust to dust and ashes to ashes." What a weird thing to say. In actual fact, Scripture teaches that we physically are basically dust, that one day we will die. The dying process will lead to a decomposition and disintegration, and we will return to the dust from which we've come.

Why does the Bible talk in these terms? A full-grown human body is composed of about fifty-eight pounds of oxygen, two ounces of salt, fifty quarts of water, three pounds of calcium, and twenty-four ounces of carbon, with a little chlorine, phosphorus, fat, iron, sulfur, and glycerin thrown in. That's you; that's me. The process of life will bring me to the point of death. Decomposition will set in; I came from dust, and that's what I'll return to. This is reality.

This idea of coming from dust and returning to dust was impressed on a little boy in Sunday school one day. That evening he was having prayer time with his mother and knelt by his bed. He wasn't really concentrating while she was praying. She nudged him and told him it was his time to pray, and he said, "Lord, all I can say is, I just looked under the bed, and there's somebody either coming or going there."

Our demise, however, which is eventual and inevitable, is divinely controlled: "You [God] turn men back to dust." God brought us into being, sustains us in our being, and will take us out of being. He is Adonai, the controller and sustainer of the universe, including you and me.

The Reality of Evil

Next the psalmist reflects on the basic issue of the reality of evil before the face of God.

> 7We are consumed by your anger
>   and terrified by your indignation.
> 8You have set our iniquities before you,
>   our secret sins in the light of your presence.
> 9All our days pass away under your wrath;
>   we finish our years with a moan.

This isn't pleasant reading, but it's reality. There is a connection between God's sweeping people away into death and our being consumed by his anger. By one person's wrongdoing, sin entered into the world, and death entered the world by sin, so there is an inextricable link between sin and death. If you think of eternity, then you have to think of the brevity of life, which leads to thinking of death, from which you must give consideration to evil.

Of course, people are very happy to talk about "evil" in a general sense because there's considerable agreement on the subject. Everybody that I know would agree that, when twenty million people were slaughtered in China in the Maoist Cultural Revolution, that was evil gone berserk. Everybody I know says that when twenty million people were killed in Stalin's reign of terror in the Soviet Union, that was unmitigated evil. They will even say that when eleven million people were slaughtered in the Holocaust in

Europe in the 1930s and 1940s that was obviously evil. And when in the space of three months in 1994 one million Rwandans were slaughtered by their own fellow nationals, that was evil.

So we have no problem talking about evil in the abstract or on a grand scale. People talk about "society being evil" or the "evils of society," and they see the solution in societal engineering. They seem to overlook the rather obvious fact that society is made up exclusively of people. If society is evil, the reason is that people are evil in a concrete sense.

In his remarkable book *The Gulag Archipelago*, Aleksandr Solzhenitsyn came to an understanding of the evil in his own heart:

> In the intoxication of youthful success I had felt myself infallible, and I was therefore cruel. In the surfeit of power I was a murderer and an oppressor. In my most evil moments I was convinced I was doing good. It was only when I lay there on my rotting prison straw that I sensed within myself the first stirrings of good. Gradually it was disclosed to me that the line separating good and evil passes not through states, nor between classes, nor between parties either—but right through every human heart.

We can all see evil clearly when we look at one class prejudiced against another, or one political party opposed to another. But Solzhenitsyn goes further, saying there is a line between good and evil in my own heart too. The psalmist would say, "Amen, Solzhenitsyn. What took you so long? If you'd read Psalm 90, you would have understood that death and evil are related." Death is God's judgment on human sin, and human sin is the iniquity and "secret sin" that must be evaluated "in the light of [God's] presence" (vs. 8).

Who decides what is evil? Who decides what is good?

Who decides what is right or what is wrong? The Lord, *Adonai,* alone is the One, who in the light of his presence, determines what is evil and what is sinful. He is the One who examines the heart of the individual.

The Misery of Humanity

Verses 9-11 describe the misery of humanity as it relates to the fall:

> 9All our days pass away under your wrath;
>   we finish our years with a moan.
> 10The length of our days is seventy years—
>   or eighty, if we have the strength;
> yet their span is but trouble and sorrow,
>   for they quickly pass, and we fly away.

> 11Who knows the power of your anger?
>   For your wrath is as great as the fear that is due
>   you.

"Who knows the power of your anger?" the psalmist asks. Good question. What human being adequately understands the righteous, just indignation of God? Nobody. Did you know that, as a result of human sin, our world is fallen? Did you know that there is evidence of fallenness on every hand? Did you know that you can no more escape breathing in the fallenness of our world than you can fail to breathe in smog in Los Angeles?

The first three chapters of the book of Genesis are amplified in Romans 1 and 5, where we have explained to us that the judgment of God is being revealed against human sin. The result is fallen individuals, relationships, cultures, the physical realm, ecology—fallenness on every side. There is a strand of depravity through it all. If we haven't grasped that, we haven't begun to grasp what it means to be human.

When we look at the sorrow and the trouble, the moans and the groans, we would like to hear people saying, "We're in this predicament because we live in a fallen universe that is directly related to human evil and divine judgment." If it is true that the line between good and evil goes right through the middle of my heart, that I live in a fallen world that is under God's judgment, that I come from dust and I return to dust, and that my life is incredibly brief in the light of eternity, it's about time I got my act together.

A Heart of Wisdom

To learn how to "number our days," we need hearts of wisdom; we need to turn to the Lord and hear from him. The last section of Psalm 90 expresses this truth.

12Teach us to number our days aright,
   that we may gain a heart of wisdom.

13Relent, O Lord! How long will it be?
   Have compassion on your servants.
14Satisfy us in the morning with your unfailing love,
   that we may sing for joy and be glad all our days.
15Make us glad for as many days as you have afflicted
   us,
   for as many years as we have seen trouble.
16May your deeds be shown to your servants,
   your splendor to their children.

17May the favor of the Lord our God rest upon us;
   establish the work of our hands for us—
   yes, establish the work of our hands.

When we turn to the Lord seeking a heart of wisdom, what do we ask for? Compassion, unfailing love, and the joy and gladness only he can give (vss. 13-14). What do we pray for? That his deeds might be manifest in our lives (vs. 16). When we turn to the Lord, what is it that we're seeking? That he would touch us in daily life so that the very work of our hands would be done to his eternal glory (vs. 17).

We can be certain that God will touch us, because nearly two thousand years ago, there was a cross, on which God in Christ—Adonai, controller and sustainer of the universe—assumed the consequences of our sin. He passed judgment on sin, and he paid the fine for sin. He did it for you, and he did it for me. You'll find God when you admit your sin, turn from it, submit yourself to his lordship, and discover his loving, gracious forgiveness. Then the strange stirrings of new inner desires will begin—a heart of wisdom that begins to see things from God's perspective, to desire things as he desires them, and that is infused with new ability through the presence of the risen Christ in the person of the Holy Spirit.

Is this just a theological statement? No. It works practically, day by day, as you say, "Lord, in the light of eternity I don't have an awful lot of time; but today I've got a pair of hands that are available to you, and I've got a heart that throbs with love for you, empowered by your Spirit, that is being touched by wisdom from above. So, Lord, send me to work and establish the work of my hands today. And may my life glorify you and do something of lasting eternal significance."

One of the things I love about the Bible is that it deals with such vast subjects as God's everlasting existence. It addresses such great mysteries as death and evil, and it brings everything right down to a personal relationship with a living God that shows itself in the way we go about our daily work. What more could we wish for?

It would probably be true to say that some of us are not "numbering our days." We are not taking time out to reaffirm our basic beliefs. Accordingly, we do not reflect on basic issues of life and fail to recognize our basic need for God. Consequently, it may be that we haven't gotten our act together.

It's so easy to fill our lives with trivialities. But God calls us to something higher and nobler and grander. In the light of eternity, and in the face of evil and sin, he wants to put us in touch with that love and compassion demonstrated in Jesus Christ. He wants to lead us to repentance and faith and infuse us with the grace of his Spirit. That's living wisely.

11

The Upright Heart

Psalm 119

In his monumental exposition of the Psalms aptly titled *The Treasury of David,* Charles Haddon Spurgeon devoted no less than 398 pages of small type to Psalm 119. He said of this lengthy chapter in the Bible, "It contains no idle word. . . . It is loaded with holy sense and is as weighty as it is bulky."

I recommend reading through Psalm 119 at one sitting. As you do, notice the many references to the heart. It's also interesting to note that this psalm is an alphabetic acrostic. There are twenty-two stanzas that correspond to the twenty-two letters in the Hebrew alphabet. Each eight-line stanza begins with a different letter of the Hebrew alphabet (in alphabetic order). This is a very skillful piece of literature. But it is much more than that.

In this psalm—the longest psalm and, indeed, the longest chapter of the Bible—practically every verse mentions in one way or another the Scriptures, the Word of God. Clearly this is a psalm in praise of the Word of God and in praise of the life that accrues to those who live in the light of God's Word with upright hearts.

Upright or Uptight?

We will look only at the first stanza of Psalm 119 which describes people with upright hearts.

¹Blessed are they whose ways are blameless,
　　who walk according to the law of the LORD.
²Blessed are they who keep his statutes
　　and seek him with all their heart.
³They do nothing wrong;
　　they walk in his ways.
⁴You have laid down precepts
　　that are to be fully obeyed.
⁵Oh, that my ways were steadfast
　　in obeying your decrees!
⁶Then I would not be put to shame
　　when I consider all your commands.
⁷I will praise you with an upright heart
　　as I learn your righteous laws.
⁸I will obey your decrees;
　　do not utterly forsake me.

This psalm tells us that when we respond appropriately to God's Word, our lives are profoundly affected. Scripture begins to produce in us what the psalmist calls an "upright heart" (vs. 7). Not up*tight*, but upright. Some people confuse the two, thinking that if you're going to be upright, then you've got to be uptight. But that is not the case at all. Joyful living and a righteous heart are not mutually exclusive.

Let me define what an upright heart is. The Hebrew word for *upright* means literally "to go straight." The Philistines, hated enemies of the Israelites, had stolen the Ark of the Covenant. The Ark held the Law and was the center of worship for the children of Israel. When the thieves had serious problems as a result, they decided they'd better return it. So they put it on a cart pulled by two cows, which they set off to return the Ark. We read that the animals "went straight up toward Beth Shemesh; . . . *they did not turn to the right or to the left*" (1 Sam. 6:12, italics mine).

The same is true of the person with an upright heart: he or she does not turn to the right or to the left, but goes straight ahead. This is not a political statement. It is a statement concerning the way that people conduct their lives.

Hope for the Deviant Heart

The problem, however, is that the heart, according to what Jeremiah 17:9 tells us, is "deceitful above all things and beyond cure." That's not terribly encouraging; in fact it almost seems to cancel out any hope of an upright heart. But the prophet continues, "Heal me, O LORD, and I will be healed; save me and I will be saved, for you are the one I praise" (vs. 14).

Of course the human heart is deviant, devious, and deceitful, and no human being or philosophy, no human structure or invention can cure the human heart. But here is the good news: it is God who heals; it is God who saves. When we begin to see his work in our lives, we discover a deviant heart that begins desiring and doing that which is right. The crooked heart, as it were, goes straight and becomes an upright heart.

Some of you may not be inclined to agree that you have a deviant heart. As we learned in our examination of the steadfast heart in chapter 9, the *heart* is not just the seat of the emotions. The heart is the center of the mind, the emotions, and the will—the part of us that discerns, desires, and decides. Would it be true to say that sometimes we don't discern things correctly? Of course it would.

Would it be true to say that sometimes we desire things that are wrong? Of course it is true. Do we find ourselves sometimes deciding to do things, knowing full well that we won't do them, and sometimes deciding we'll never do a thing again, yet have every intention of doing it again? We all know this hypocrisy is true. When we find this ambivalence in ourselves, then we know we have deviant, deceitful hearts.

If, therefore, we're thinking seriously about gaining an upright heart, we must first recognize that it is deviant. We must also recognize that nothing human beings can do will cure it; only God can. The question is, do we really want that to happen? It is one thing to define an upright heart, but it's an entirely different thing to desire it. The fact of the matter is that, given our own deviousness, often we know what is true but prefer what is in error. Sometimes truth is uncomfortable, so we will choose the lie.

Unfortunately, because of our fallenness we know that there are desires within us at the most inopportune times that are totally unconscionable. We would be embarrassed to death if anybody knew about them, and we know that we shouldn't desire them. But guess what? We will go on desiring them anyway and probably excuse ourselves and simply say, "Of course, it's addictive behavior." The apostle Paul wrote about his own experience of this struggle, "For what I do is not the good I want to do; no, the evil I do not want to do—this I keep on doing" (Rom. 7:19). What will it take, then, for us to truly have an upright heart?

Blessed to Be a Blessing

Psalm 119 starts out with "Blessed are they whose ways are blameless, . . . Blessed are they who keep his statutes" (vss. 1, 2). In its simplest form, *to bless* means "to impart favor and good." We use the term quite accurately and not infrequently in our normal conversation. I once heard the defensive coordinator of the Green Bay Packers talking about some new players that they'd signed: "The good Lord has blessed them with being 300 pounds." Or we hear a marvelous singer and say, "God blessed her with a wonderful voice." *God* blessed them. God imparted. God gave. God favored.

But to bless can also communicate that, now that I understand that God has favored me, *I* can bless *his* name. So I sing, "Bless the Lord, O my soul, and all that is within me, bless his holy name." What does that mean? I speak well of him because I have discovered his great goodness and favor in my life.

Sometimes we talk about a "blessing" before a meal. We bow our heads and ask a blessing. What are we asking? We're asking that God through this provision would impart his favor to us. At the same time, we are blessing him for his great goodness and favor to us.

So what does it mean to be blessed? First, blessed people are *conscious of God's goodness and favor in their lives.* They are excited about this and live in such a way that they are thanking, praising, and blessing God. Moreover, having experienced blessing in their lives, they also seek to bring blessing to others.

Second, blessed people are *integrated people*—"together" people in everyday language. In verse 1 we read, "Blessed are they whose ways are blameless, who walk according to the law of the LORD." Don't get too alarmed with this term *blameless.* It doesn't mean faultless or absolutely perfect, but rather complete, balanced, and integrated. They have been able to bring the physical, emotional, spiritual, and intellectual aspects of their lives into harmony.

Perhaps you say, "My life is all over the place. It's coming apart at the seams." Then you notice another person who is not immune to difficulties but seems to be able to handle them a lot better than you could. The reason may be found in the second verse: "They . . . keep [God's] statutes and seek him with all their heart." Their knowledge and experience of God come together in their actions. We must come to God's Word with a deep spiritual hunger and openness in order to be integrated people.

Third, blessed people *do what is right.* "They do nothing wrong; they walk in his ways" (vs. 3). Here again, this doesn't mean they're perfect. It means that in their relationships and in their social activities they have a tremendous commitment to doing that which is right, just, and fair.

What's the point of all this? You only become a blessed person when you know what it is to be upright in heart. And it is only because you are blessed by God that you discover that your deviant heart is beginning to go straight. You begin to desire the uprightness, you begin to desire the blessedness, because you know that's what life is all about.

It's very difficult to persuade some people that they should do what they know is true rather than what they know feels good. Somewhere along the line we need a work of grace in our lives that is going to touch our devious hearts and instill in us the desire to live the blessed life, to glorify God, to affect other people positively, and to discover a depth of riches and resources we never knew possible. If we begin to see the attractiveness, the winsomeness, and the value of the blessed life, it will lead us to desire the upright heart.

Growing an Upright Heart

Let's assume, for the sake of argument, that we are clear in our definition of an upright heart and have an inner aspiration for it. How do we develop such a heart? Clearly, Psalm 119 points us to a right relationship with God's Word as the key. I am not suggesting that you simply stick your nose in the Bible and memorize it all. Three things are necessary: we need to *appreciate* God's Word, *approach* God's Word, and then *apply* it.

Appreciate God's Word.

What do I mean by appreciating God's Word? I mean that we need to look at our true heart attitude toward the Scriptures. God's Word is his personal revelation of himself, a résumé of his purposes, and a resource for his people. The one who believes these things are true is appreciating the opportunity the Word of God affords to know who God is, what he plans, and what he offers.

For example, when asked in one of our omnipresent polls, "Do you believe the Bible is the Word of God?" the vast majority of people on the North American continent say "Yes." Yet if you were to ask them, "How much time do you spend in it?" the answer would be, "Very little." Here is a very strange thing. How can somebody say with a straight face the Bible is the Word of God but to all intents and purposes ignore it? If I really believe it is the Word of God, I am going to hunger for it and make sure that in my busy life I make time for it. A reverence for the Word does not necessarily or automatically translate into reading it, marking it, learning it. We must also believe it, obey it, and see it transform our lives. What keeps us from appreciating God's Word fully? The answer can usually be found in how we approach the Bible.

Approach God's Word as truth.

Modernism, a philosophical school of thought or world view developed in the eighteenth century, posited that human beings have the rational capability to evaluate everything. From this grew the scientific method and then much of our modern technology. In their arrogance, these people determined that unless something could be proved by the scientific method using empirical approaches, it was not true. They of course concluded that they could not scientifically evaluate claims to miracles, so miracles and the supernatural were dismissed as not possible. They developed a Bible that got rid of a supernatural God and that was inadequate to reveal anything that their intellect could not contain. They developed preachers and seminaries that emasculated the Word of God. I'll guarantee that one of the reasons that a lot of people today don't take the Bible seriously is that they have bought into modernistic thinking without even knowing it.

Postmodernism in the twentieth century goes even further astray and assumes that there is no absolute truth, so why bother arguing how to find it? Everything is relative. If everything is relative, it is perfectly obvious that the Bible cannot contain absolute truth, for there is no such thing as absolute truth. Postmodernism includes the "feel good" approach to Scripture. This says that if what I read makes me feel good, it will be fine; but if I don't like it then I won't believe it. If the Bible talks about hell and I don't like that idea, I'll believe the Bible but just won't believe in hell. If the Bible says that God is a God of fierce anger as well as of unconditional love but I don't like the anger part, I'll believe that he's a God of unconditional love but ignore the fierce anger aspect of his character.

Ask yourself, What is my attitude toward the Bible? How do I approach it? Do I revere it but ignore it? Am I a modernist who determines on the basis of my own intellect what is acceptable or unacceptable? Am I a postmodernist who simply says there's no such thing as absolute truth; that this may be true for you and that may be true for me, but ultimately it is a matter of how we feel at the moment?

Decide in your own heart. Be strictly honest with yourself about it. The Bible tells us in no uncertain terms that it is a revelation of God himself that is to be delighted in, not dissected; to be embraced with joy rather than treated with selective indifference.

Apply God's Word.

The Bible also claims to be a resource for God's people to apply in their lives. It will give us commands to obey and promises to claim. It will give us comfort for broken hearts. It will give us rebuke for rebellious attitudes. It will give us instruction when we're ignorant. It will give us guidance, direction, and encouragement when we're down.

The Word is a rich resource for us. Ask yourself, Do I come to God's Word believing it to be inspired by the Spirit, made available in my own language with umpteen versions sitting on my shelf? Because I am convinced that it is God's self-revelation, am I going to make sure that I read it, learn it, inwardly digest it, obey it, and live in it so that it lives in me, by God's Spirit?

Change from the Inside Out

If you appreciate, approach, and apply the Bible rightly, you will find the grace of God beginning to change you from the inside out. An old saying states: "The Bible will keep you from sin, or sin will keep you from the Bible." Which is true of your life? Is this Word of God, empowered by the Spirit of God, alive in your heart? Is it keeping you from sin, turning your deviant heart into an upright heart? Is it making you live the blessed life? Or is sin in your life allowing you to make all kinds of excuses so that you don't get into God's Word?

What an irony that the Soviet Union, devised on a communistic structure based on human rationality to solve human beings' problems, collapsed because the structure didn't work. What an irony that now there are thousands of public schools asking for people to come in and teach them principles of morals and ethics based on the Bible. What an irony that in America there are people with Bibles on their shelves that they never bother to open. What an irony that there are "Bible-believing" Christians who never take the time to study the Bible or share it.

In the words of Psalm 119, may we be a people "whose ways are blameless, who walk according to the law of the LORD." May the world see a people who are blessed because we seek him with all our hearts.

12

The Humble Heart

Psalm 131

In this final chapter, we will explore humility—a most significant dimension of the heart and a complex part of our humanity. As we have searched the Psalms to learn more about our inner selves, we have been reminded constantly that the only appropriate attitude of the believer is one of humility. So it is right that we conclude with the psalmist's heartfelt claim, "My heart is not proud, O Lord." May we be able to echo his words!

False Humility?

In only three brief verses, Psalm 131 teaches us some very significant things about the heart and humility.

> ¹My heart is not proud, O LORD,
>   my eyes are not haughty;
> I do not concern myself with great matters
>   or things too wonderful for me.
> ²But I have stilled and quieted my soul;
>   like a weaned child with its mother,
>   like a weaned child is my soul within me.

³O Israel, put your hope in the LORD
both now and forevermore.

Can you say with the psalmist that your heart isn't proud? Can you honestly say that you feel humble? Albert Einstein once wrote, "Everyone who is seriously involved in the pursuit of science becomes convinced that a spirit is manifest in the laws of the universe. A spirit in the face of which we, with our modest powers, must feel humble." Here was a scientist who was in touch with the vastness of the universe and saw himself in comparison to it. He sensed that he was dealing with things beyond his comprehension, beyond his control, beyond his understanding, and he bowed humbly before them.

When you think about it, the psalmist's statement in verse 1 seems almost self-contradictory, doesn't it? It sounds as though he was declaring, "Take a good look. I'm not proud. Here's a very humble person." We'd be turned off immediately and assume this person had a pride problem.

But notice to whom the psalmist, David, says these words: "My heart is not proud, O LORD." He's not going around talking to his friends, and he's not looking in the mirror talking to himself. He has drawn aside and come quietly before the Lord. He is doing the most dangerous thing imaginable—baring his soul before God and opening his heart to the scrutiny of the Lord. He is saying, "Lord, as you know my heart, I am not proud."

What a remarkable thing to be able to say. Why would the psalmist be talking like this? Why is he going to God to assure himself that his heart is not proud? Let's look again at some events in David's life.

Lessons from David

You remember when he was a youngster, David went down to see his brothers who were in the army. The armies

of the Philistines were confronting the armies of the Israelites, and the giant Goliath was challenging them. Young
David was intrigued with Goliath and asked some of the
soldiers, "Why doesn't someone accept Goliath's challenge
and go fight him? Would there not be some advantage to
that?"

The soldiers replied, "Oh yes, there would. Major finan-
cial rewards offered to anybody. The king says the man
can marry one of his daughters. In addition, his family will
be excused from income taxes for the rest of their lives."
Excellent incentives, but nobody was about to tackle Goliath. When David's older brother Eliab heard about
David's inquiries, he said, "Listen, David, you're just far
too conceited and big-headed. You think you can do something that nobody else can do. Why don't you go back and
look after your sheep?" (See 1 Sam. 17:17-30.)

Those remarks went deep with David. Sometimes when
negative motives and pride are attributed to us wrongly,
we can fight it, but the hurt is still there. In the end the
only thing we can do is go before the Lord and say, "Help
me to examine my heart. They don't know what's going
on. Is it true that I am conceited? Is it true that my heart
is proud?"

Much later in life King David managed to rescue the Ark
of the Covenant and bring it back to Jerusalem. He was
so excited that he organized and led a big religious procession and festival, complete with musicians and a choir.
David got so excited that he started to dance, which can
happen if the music sort of gets into your feet. It was a
little difficult dancing because he had on all his majestic,
kingly robes. So he just took them off. In front of the
whole crowd he started dancing and thoroughly worship-
ing the Lord, wearing only a linen ephod.

His wife, who was looking out of the palace, expressed
her disgust. "You're not supposed to behave like that in
worship," she told him. "You're supposed to be proper
and correct and not allow your emotions to show. You

are like one of those vulgar fellows."

He responded, "I wasn't dancing for you. And I wasn't dancing for the rest of them. I was dancing before the Lord. So you can think what you like about my motives—they were genuine and honest. I was humbling myself before the Lord." (See 2 Samuel 6.)

So some people criticized him for being too conceited, and others criticized him for being too humble. What do you do in a situation like that? You take a risk, come before the Lord, and say, "Please help me examine my heart. Is it true that I have a humble heart?"

Is Humility a Virtue?

What is the significance of humility? In William Bennett's *The Book of Virtues,* you will not find humility listed as one of the virtues. The reason is that Bennett draws his list of virtues from the ancient Greek philosophers, and they did not think humility was a virtue. In fact, the Greeks despised humility in much the same way as many people do today. They assumed that meekness meant weakness.

But if you look in your Bible, you'll discover that humility is an important virtue. Turning the coin, you'll discover that pride is one of the worst things of which a human being can be accused. In fact, God goes so far as to say, "I hate pride and arrogance" (Prov 8:13). Why? Because pride tends to deify self. We tend to put ourselves, in our pride, in the place of God.

When Ezekiel was prophesying, there was a king of Tyre who had a bit of a big head. So the Lord told Ezekiel to tell the ruler of Tyre, "In the pride of your heart you say 'I am a god; I sit on the throne of a god in the heart of the seas.' But you are a man and not a god, though you think you are as wise as a god" (Ezek. 28:2).

Perhaps you think that pride is not a problem nowadays, and that no one goes around thinking he or she is a god. Are you sure? I meet people practically every day of the week who think they know better than God. They assume that when God says something it is not relevant to them. They have the right to decide that what God says does not apply as far as their lives are concerned. They have superior insights to God. They have assumed that in some way they are capable of managing their own affairs without God, regardless of what he says. Those people need to be reminded of something: they have a pride problem.

Better Than the Apes

Time magazine once had a particularly fascinating cover article. The front cover was basically black, with a big, broken wedding ring set against it. The large type underneath it read "Infidelity." Then in smaller letters was the phrase "may be in our genes." I wondered how the magazine had arrived at that conclusion, so I read the article.

The basic assumption was that, if we are to understand our humanity, we should evaluate and understand the behavior of the primates because we are closely related to them. Scientists had evaluated the sexual habits and certain physical attributes of chimpanzees, orangutans, apes, and gorillas. They concluded that there was a direct correlation between the physical attributes and the degree of sexual faithfulness of the primates. Then they figured out where we physiologically fit in the continuum between the chimpanzee and the gorilla and assumed that our behavior will be related to our physical attributes because, basically, we are just a little higher than the apes.

The assumption that we are just a little higher than the apes is erroneous because God says we're a little lower than the angels (Ps. 8:5). If you decide to simply ignore this truth and ignore that God has ordained standards of behavior, then you will behave one way. If you think you simply know better than God and say, "I don't want to regard myself as a little lower than the angels created by God for a specific purpose. I prefer to believe that I have simply evolved into something far superior to the apes, and I can look around at the rest of creation and say, 'I am superior.'" God looks down from heaven and says, "Wrong." The essence of pride is the innate tendency to deify self.

Looking Down Our Noses

There is another problem with pride. Notice that the psalmist says, "My heart is not proud, O LORD, my eyes are not haughty." Haughtiness has to do with the way we look at other people. We tend sometimes to look down our noses at others. Then, having decided that we are better than they are, we are full of superior feelings. We take the logical next step of assuming that we are all right with God. How illogical can you get?

Our world is full of people who, if you ask, "Do you think you'll go to heaven when you die?" will say yes. If you ask them, "Why in the world would God want you in his heaven?" they'll say, "Because I was better than her or him." It's hard to understand why that would be relevant, but the tendency for some is to assume that they are all right and acceptable because they have measured themselves against other people. They have haughty eyes.

Jesus once told a striking story about two men who went up to the temple to pray. One of them was a very humble man, and he bowed himself before the Lord and said, "Lord, be merciful to me, a sinner." That's humility, in case you weren't sure how to describe it. The other man, however, didn't approach it that way. He prayed to himself and said, "God, I thank you I am not like other men." That's the essence of arrogance—deifying himself, looking down on other people, and assuming that there's nothing wrong with his life.

The seriousness of this situation needs to be appreciated. You see, the Bible does not teach that we are superior, or that we have evolved into a position that is markedly better than all the other evolved creatures in our world. The Bible teaches that there is behind all things a sovereign Lord, from whom we come and to whom we are accountable. If I accept this, then I must ask myself not "What do I think of me?" or "What do you think of me?" but "What does *God* think of me?"

In our Bible school in England there was a retired missionary named Fred Train. He was a wonderful, down-to-earth character who had worked among the Indians of Paraguay for many years. On one occasion a young student came to talk to him and said, "Mr. Train, I would like you to know my father thinks that, given my intellect and my training, it would be a total waste for me to be a missionary." Fred looked at him and said, "How interesting. I would rather like to know what God thinks of your father."

It is far more important what God thinks of me than what I think of what God has said. But many today sit in judgment on God and resent and resist any suggestion that God sits in judgment on them. If it is true that the Lord is sovereign and we are his creation, let's ask him, "What do you expect of me?" The answer, of course, comes loudly and clearly in the prophet Micah. "With what shall I come before the LORD and bow down before the exalted God?" he asks. "He has showed you . . . what is good. And what does the LORD require of you? To act justly and to love mercy and to walk humbly with your God" (Micah 6, 8).

In other words, there is a sovereign God by whom and for whom we were created, who designed us for dependence and obedience. But we prefer independence and relish disobedience; this is the essence of pride. We maneuver ourselves into a position of self-deification. We look with a supercilious attitude at people whom we assume are worse than us and regard ourselves as the center of the universe. God reminds us, "No way. I am God." And we must humble ourselves before him.

An Honest Approach to Knowing

The psalmist goes on to explain in a little more detail what he means by humility. "I do not concern myself with great matters or things too wonderful for me. But I have stilled and quieted my soul" (vss. 1-2). This does not mean he checked in his brains at the door. This is not an anti-intellectual statement. God requires us to worship him with all our being, including our minds. So the psalmist is saying, "I have come to the point of a humble appraisal of human limitations. There are great matters beyond my knowing."

Many modern people assume that the only things that are true are those things which can be evaluated by the scientific method and which fit within the confines of human intellect. Thus, human intellect and reason determine truthfulness. How arrogant can you get?

Let me give you an entirely different approach. Deuteronomy 29:29 says, "The secret things belong to the Lord our God, but the things revealed belong to us and to our children forever, that we may follow all the words of this law." In other words, we know some things, but we don't know everything.

Which is the better approach to knowing: to say that unless a thing is verifiable it cannot be true and, accordingly, all that is true can be confined within human intellect? Or would it be more accurate to say that there is a God behind all things, who has chosen to reveal certain things and has chosen not to reveal other things? I therefore humbly bow before him and use my intellect to understand what he has revealed, and I will humbly admit that my intellect is totally incapable of grasping many of the things that are knowable only by him. In other words, am I proud or am I humble?

Some people struggle between whether to use their intellect or just be creatures of faith. Many think that to be a believer means they must commit intellectual suicide.

But we do not believe because we *see;* in actual fact, we see *because* we believe. (For example, after Jesus rose from the dead he appeared to his disciples, and they thought they'd seen a ghost. Why? Because they believed in ghosts and didn't believe in resurrections.) Anselm, the early church father, put it well when he said, "I believe in order to understand."

"My heart is not proud," said the psalmist. He did not concern himself with great matters because he was perfectly comfortable accepting the fact that knowledge is totally dependent on divine revelation. Consider the story of the seal of Harvard University, formerly Harvard College—formed explicitly for the training of men for the Christian ministry. The original seal had three open books on it; two of them were facing out so you could read them, and one was face down so you couldn't read it. The image communicated the biblical truth that there are many things human beings can understand, but there are certain things that are hidden and only God can reveal. Today the seal is different. Somewhere along the line they turned the other book over. No one likes to think they are dependent on God's revelation.

A Sense of Wonder

G. K. Chesterton wrote, "The world will never starve for want of wonders, but only for want of wonder." There's a marked shortage in people today of awe and wonder.

Once I listened to a televised debate on whether abortion should be included in health care packages. The focus was on the autonomy of the individual to determine what is right or wrong, with no sense of what God says. They had lost the sense of wonder at the miracle of conception and birth. For years Dr. Jack Kevorkian helped people commit suicide. He had lost a sense of wonder and awe for the mystery of life. He argued that we have the absolute right not to suffer.

From where do we get that right? Such thinking comes from the autonomy of the individual, the deification of the self. However, there's a God from whom we come and to whom we go, and we can listen to him and find that he is the One who gives life. If he allows us to suffer, he doesn't just sit there with his arms crossed. He points to the cross of Jesus and says, "I understand your suffering. I suffered myself."

What has happened to our sense of the wonder of life? What has happened to our sense of the mystery of death? What has happened to our grasp of salvation—the wonder of God in grace reaching out to people totally undeserving of him? The wonder of God in Christ dying on the cross and bearing our sin, the sheer wonder of God raising Christ from the dead and giving the assurance of life after death, and the sheer wonder of his sending his Spirit into our hearts and lives to transform us? Without wonder, we are doomed to human arrogance and folly.

Humble Like a Child

Finally the psalmist says, "But I have stilled and quieted my soul; like a weaned child with its mother, like a weaned child is my soul within me." In those days, a child was weaned at the age of three. By the time a child is three and is used to deriving great comfort from the mother's breast, they were less than enthusiastic about being denied it. Therefore the process was very fractious, but eventually mother and child came through it. Then the child would just rest on the mother's breast.

What a picture of the infantile struggle of so many people—assuming they know better than God, refusing to depend, refusing to obey, insisting on their own way. We go through the frenetic time, and then the day comes when we can trust and quiet our souls and rest upon the One whose will we've resisted. We trust the one we've resented.

Having come to this place of humility, the psalmist then

turns to the rest of the people and says, "O Israel, put your hope in the LORD both now and forevermore." If we are to live in the now rightly, we do it humbly, obediently, trusting a gracious God who in Christ gives us all we need. And if ever we're to know life in the forever, the same attitudes must be ours. That is our message.

Up Is Down

When I was a teenager, my parents dragged me to the Keswick Convention, a Bible conference. I was sitting there in the back row in a big tent on a hot summer afternoon, determined not to listen. I was shaken out of my resistant reverie when the speaker got up and, without any introduction whatsoever, bellowed at the top of his voice, "The way to up is down! And the way to down is up!" He was the famous American preacher Donald Grey Barnhouse. I didn't know who he was and I don't remember his sermon, but I never, ever escaped from what he said.

His words were a paraphrase of what Peter said: "'God opposes the proud but gives grace to the humble.' Humble yourselves, therefore, under God's mighty hand, that he may lift you up in due time" (1 Pet. 5:5-6). Some of us think we can make ourselves fit for heaven. Some of us think we are better than others. Some of us are in utter confusion and resisting God. May God help us humbly turn to him, recognizing our need of the grace he offers. The way to up is down, and the way to down is up. God will see to it.

A number of years ago my doctor recommended that I should undergo a medical procedure called a heart catheterization. The cardiologist opened an artery in my arm, fed a catheter with a tiny camera attached into my heart, and explored my arteries. It was quite exciting to watch my own heart on a television monitor. (Now when people accuse me of being heartless, I know better!) Just as the wonders of modern science allow us to see into our cardiac system, so the wonders of God's Word give insight into our inner hearts. May we learn well from what we see there and always turn to our Eternal Cardiologist, the God who is our refuge and strength.

Tapes Available

A complete listing of audiotaped messages by Stuart Briscoe is available from:

> Telling the Truth
> Elmbrook Church
> 777 South Barker Road
> Brookfield, WI 53045
>
> 800-24-TRUTH
> Fax: 414-796-5752
> Website: www.tellingthetruth.org

Further studies on the psalms are available in Stuart Briscoe's book *What Works When Life Doesn't*, available from Shaw Publishers.